Is a Culture of Life Still Possible in the United States?

Is a Culture of Life Still Possible in the United States?

Proceedings from
the Twentieth Convention of
The Fellowship of Catholic Scholars

Washington, D.C.
1997

Rev. Anthony J. Mastroeni, S.T.D., J.D.
Editor

ST. AUGUSTINE'S PRESS
South Bend, Indiana
1999

 Fellowship of Catholic Scholars

Table of Contents

PART I

Public Policy
in the
Recent Catholic Tradition

Public Philosophy in the Recent Catholic Tradition

Deal W. Hudson
Crisis Magazine

The attempt to articulate and promulgate a Catholic public philosophy in contemporary America has been largely a failure. Why? For those of us who followed the Catholic vote closely, in the 1996 presidential election one empirical fact kept presenting itself. The so-called "Catholic vote" was really not distinguishable from the general voting block. If you wonder why Dole and the Republican Party never responded to "pro-life" Catholic pressure, it was because they had good reason to believe there was no great advantage to carrying a pro-life banner.

It soon became apparent that the only concrete reasons to target the Catholic block was its size (nearly thirty-five percent of those who vote), and its obvious susceptibility to institutional sentimentality. Evidently all it took was a few newspaper photos of the first family in soup kitchens surrounded by clerical collars to sway the 3.5 percent of voters in the mid-western Catholic states crucial to re-election.

Direct public challenges to Clinton's abortion message from the Holy Father on the tarmac at the Denver airport, or by Mother Teresa herself at the prayer breakfast, had no discernible effect. The self-identified Catholic vote, it turns out, is largely indistinguishable from the non-Catholic vote in this Protestant country.

American Catholics, while having an ethnic profile, have no distinctive ethical profile. All who waited for some kind of popular backlash against Clinton's veto of the partial birth abortion ban waited in vain. The cardinals and bishops who, 23 years after *Roe v. Wade,* took to the Capitol steps saying, "Enough is enough!", must have been stunned to find their compelling gesture all but ignored by the media. A belated post-card campaign caused only a ripple of attention in Congress.

Some would argue that I am giving too much attention to the abortion issue and too little attention to matters of social and economic justice, to which Catholics have historically made a great contribution, most notably through the Labor movement. I don't think this objection has much force anymore, if it ever did, for the simple reason that the distinctive Catholic basis of these rights and justice claims was never clearly articulated or understood by Catholics. No distinctive Catholic position on economic justice has been generally accepted. At present, it is largely indistinguishable from the platform of the Democratic party, with only a few established Catholics coming forward to offer any regrets over the failure of the welfare state.

Here is not only a failure of principle, but also a failure to recognize the principles underlining the choice of means. Catholic public philosophy has been a failure because of its inability to communicate the principles grounding its claims regarding rights in a larger vision of the moral good. Principles like solidarity, subsidiarity, and the preferential option are often treated as if they were the ground floor of Catholic moral reasoning. Lacking foundational reasoning we are witnessing a spectacle of rights claims gone wild, a Dostoevskian panorama of individuals possessed by the basic belief that "right" means the moral sanction of personal preferences. It appears that Catholics over the years have simply been voting for improve-ments in their lifestyle, like everyone else.

4

Of course we shouldn't go too far in criticizing those who hold this assumption since our own Supreme Court, the *Casey* court as we have come to call it, created a right to define the meaning of existence. Thus the Constitutional order officially recognizes that there is no law or measure higher than the individual mind. How appropriate, then, that Justice Brennan was buried at St. Matthew's Cathedral in Washington, D.C. with all the attentive pomp of a Catholic ceremony.

Many of us have spent much of our lives trying to figure out what went wrong with modern culture. What forces combined to create the culture of death? We have at various times pointed our fingers at Ockham, Scotus, Luther or Descartes, Nietzsche, Freud and John Dewey have regularly come under fire, and closer to home there are the liberals we are so fond of blaming for everything that goes wrong. But I wonder if some of us and some of our own heros haven't contributed unintentionally to the present mess. I am thinking of my own mentor Jacques Maritain and, specifically, his assumption that we could postpone talking about the justification of principles among nations while agreeing on civilized norms. The failure of Catholic public philosophy, I think, represents the failure of Thomism to meet the expectations of the social promise that it displayed at mid-century.

Among Maritain's many political achievements was his collaboration on the 1948 United Nations Universal Declaration of Human Rights, which he wrote about in *Man and the State*. There he argues that, "The practical can be separated from the theoretical for the sake of political cooperation. In this case people of various religious and ideological backgrounds can agree on a list of basic human rights without agreeing on their theoretical justification. Such practical agreement is attractive since it leads to political cooperation between unlikely allies and concrete social progress among nations."

I wonder if Maritain foresaw what would happen as a result of this shelving of the theoretical for the sake of practical political cooperation. The concrete measurable progress has come at a cost. Those who knew how to provide arguments for the universality of human rights based upon natural law have either forgotten those arguments or retreated into a flabby communitarianism that is easily defeated by the multiculturalist. Those on the other side of the table, from whom we felt obligated to withhold our strongest arguments for human rights, have become well-schooled in a multiculturalism held by the contemporary western elites. Multicultural postmodernism denies the universality of human rights from the outset and reverses the priorities that a proper view of human rights establishes in the first place. Multiculturalism breeds the ethnocentrism that is gradually asserting itself in the political marketplace by those nations that no longer want to submit to a common measure of ethical behavior.

I don't know why Maritain put so much trust in this strategy. It's said he always put too much trust in thinkers on the left. But there is no doubt that the separation of the practical from the theoretical lead directly to a breakdown. Short-term progress was traded for a long-term intellectual collapse. Maritain never intended this separation to become a permanent feature of political cooperation among nations, and he foresaw what would happen if the theoretical issues were avoided for too long. As he said in Princeton in the late 50s, "A time will come when people will give up in practical existence, those values about which they no longer have any intellectual conviction." No doubt our intellectual convictions about moral matters, especially those of the natural law, have been slowly withering over the last forty years.

Throughout his career Maritain insisted that the assertion of human rights without natural law was not only incoherent but dangerous. Few situations are more wrought with danger than when the meaning of basic moral terms are cut loose from their metaphysical moorings. As Chesterton once commented, "We live in a time where the virtues, sane when kept in relationship with one another, have gone their separate ways and have gone mad."

At present, the two strongest currents of Catholic public philosophy are the liberal rationalism of the Catholic establishment and the recently emerged Christological anthropology. The application of the theories about the Trinity and Incarnation to policy and political issues is attractive in an age such as ours. Catholics have a curriculum, and it is good to hear it proclaimed. But these attempts remain largely confined to the faithful, and risk leaving them without the tools to make a highly speculative approach to practical problems truly effective. The liberal rationalism of the establishment is manifested in a number of different ways. One example is the undue emphasis now given to bishops' public policy statements. The authoritative weight of these statements is entirely out of proportion to more fundamental matters of morals and doctrine which are the proper province of their authority: Practice has started to supplant the principles that guide it. This tendency appears to be another outbreak of the theoretical agnosticism that pervaded the creation of the "human declaration." While members of the Catholic establishment are unsure of foundational doctrinal matters, they appear certain about what public policy should be adopted to address war, poverty, and crime.

When the public philosophy of the bishops is set side-by-side with recent papal encyclicals, the differences become apparent. John Paul II's encyclicals employ the richness of the Catholic tradition, scripture, theology, and natural law to bring the moral traditions of the Church to bear on the culture. The Holy Father, to be sure, does not shrink from policy statements of sorts, as is seen in his comments on the death penalty, but his statements are made in a rich context of exegesis, spirituality, and sound political theory. These encyclicals also stand in contrast to the heavily theological Christological and Trinitarian discourse that has been put forward as an antidote to the liberal and neo-conservative strains of Catholic thought. With all the richness of these new resources for Catholic culture and spirituality, this approach does little to directly help Catholic public philosophy because it prescinds from the middle level of discourse needed to mediate between the Church and the wider culture. Yet, even as I make this comment I want to add that I applaud the boldness of these theological accounts because the state of theology itself benefits so much.

The Pope's encyclicals have helped renew our public philosophy. Certainly they invite all of us to a level of discourse all too rare since the glory days of Maritain, Murray, *et. al.* I would say, however, that what is conspicuously missing in public Catholic philosophy is also missing in the Pope's own encyclicals, and that is natural theology.[1] Catholic public philosophy seen from the perspective of its social teaching has consistently affirmed the role of natural law, but natural law presupposes a natural theology. Indeed it is both natural law and natural theology that have always been the Catholic advantage in the public square. Even Ralph Reed, founder of the Christian Coalition, expressed his envy of the Catholic law tradition in a *Crisis* interview, "The Roman Catholic idiom is far more amenable and tends to be less abrasive against the democratic ear of Americans because Catholics employ natural law theology." Reed also knows how little we Catholics use our advantage of this middle range of discourse, and, like most Protestants, are left arguing about logical fallacies or the Bible.

The language of the *Declaration of Independence* is the most obvious example of what we have lost. Such a document makes the monster of Enlightenment reasoning look pretty mild compared to what we have today. The Founders were obviously willing to commit a civic theology to paper, one with an explicit natural theology rooted in nature's God. Certainly we will never be able to reassert a civic theology or even re-appropriate the founding itself without confidently affirming the terms of natural theology. The result of limiting talk about God to the expressions of faith alone has lead to the gradual bracketing of "God talk" as being either inadmissible or dismissed as out of hand.

We have been backed into a corner, actually two corners, and one is Barthian. According to Barth, when we are talking about God we should be talking out of faith, from a deposit of revealed knowledge. We shouldn't talk about God any other way or we risk consorting with people who use God for justifying things like national socialism or the divine right of kings. In other words, natural theology leads to idolatry, particularly of a political kind. Those who tire of fighting the historical arguments entailed by this charge can retreat to the secular corner with those who believe that all religious belief is essentially private, as seen in Justice Kennedy's *Lee v. Wiseman* decision of 1992. Here Justice Kennedy reads the language of the First Amendment as ruling "God talk" out of all public places even if it conforms to the language of civil religion. Our civil order, in effect, is interpreted by the Court to rule out civil religion, which in turn rules out the Founding. Thus the political uses of natural law and natural rights go begging for their theological context, thus losing their coherence and persuasive force. Natural law is deprived of its lawgiver and treated only as an epistemological doctrine. Nature's God, the guarantor of what is universal and inalienable, is banished.

The order of authority in law is thus not a piecemeal thing. Without God the most we are left with is human nature. I have tried, without much success, to derive an argument for morality based upon the distinctiveness of rational animals, but it isn't very persuasive public argument. Without natural theology, a contemporary Catholic discourse has become more and more susceptible to New Age constructs. Take, for example, the film *Contact*. Here we see a full-blown cosmology in cinematic display. It's a sad day when Carl Sagan takes over where the Thomists left off. At least Sagan understood that Kant did not completely kill our instinct to try to make sense out of cosmological issues.

9

Our need for natural theology is being filled by a kind of pseudo-mystical theology that once formed the basis of pagan religions. The astounding success of over 300,000 hardback copies sold of Neale Donald Walsh's *Conversations with God*, what I call "the worst book I ever read," is another example of pseudo-mystical theology taking center stage. The loss of natural theology not only affects theology but also affects our understanding of the Bible. James Barr's masterful Gifford Lectures on the natural theology of the Bible shows how proper biblical exegesis has to admit natural theology as part of the scriptural narrative. Once again Catholics are being reminded by Protestants of their ignored patrimony.

The loss of natural theology obviously affects natural law. Natural law needs the recognition of a lawgiver. Those who fear the return of a blind voluntarism need not conflate divine grounding with divine voluntarism. The assertion of natural theology does not lead to voluntarism since all law is chiefly the work of reason, not the will. For several years Catholic philosophers have sought to discover the good of human life apart from God, as if by being more modern we become more persuasive. Rather than planting our flag in the public square we have been forced to retreat. We have underestimated our audience and overestimated the need to concentrate our attention on the demands of an isolated academic establishment. The public wants precisely what we have left on the shelf.

None of what I am arguing for requires that our politicians and our policy experts become experts on the proof of God's existence. The kind of discourse that I am calling for does not require strict demonstration. The middle range of discourse does not apply here to rigorous demonstration. In the middle of ethical arguments we do not require people to go back to strict demonstration. We do not need *to prove* God's existence to know moral truths. In fact, it is the nature of public rhetoric that assertions of truth need not be held to strict accounting. As Plato knew, in public utterance all that is required is true opinion. One can take note of first principles in passing, call attention to them, but not explain them. To paraphrase St. Thomas in the *Summa Contra Gentiles*: "There is a natural theology that comes with just seeing order in the world, an order that leads to God. Someone who can't see God through His effects is guilty of a blameworthy stupidity." Thomas never held that natural theology could only be done by the people who are capable of providing demonstration. Yes, the demonstrative form of natural theology is the perfection of that knowledge, but the perfect, as they say, need not become the enemy of the good.

The restoration of genuine Thomism is the best bet for Catholic public philosophy. A genuine Thomism talks at many levels to many different audiences, taking full advantage of the degrees of knowledge and certainty that reason allows. Thomism requires a flexible mind, the kind of mind that can at once frustrate the academic pedants while appealing to the common sense of the common man.

Maritain remarked that Thomists should milk cows from time to time. I couldn't agree more. If we spend a little more time with our hands in milk buckets, we might be reminded that very few minds conform to the structures that modern epistemologists have placed upon them. People outside faith communities still want to talk about God, still are drawn to God through his effects, and still need God to understand their lives. If we don't get their ear, then the Carl Sagans of the world will be happy to lead us to a pagan, and thus less human, future.

Note

1.   The situation has been corrected by the encyclical *Fides et Ratio* (1998).

Public Philosophy: A Response

Patrick Lee
Franciscan University of Steubenville
Steubenville, Ohio

I shall divide my remarks on Deal Hudson's talk into four comments. First, I am in agreement with Hudson when he cites the importance of the Catholic view on the integrity of the natural order. That is, it is proper to appeal to reason and one need not to insist on faith as a condition of cooperation or understanding. The Catholic tradition has always emphasized that grace perfects nature, it does not destroy it. This theological doctrine has important political consequences. It means that we need not insist that those with whom we cooperate first make a commitment of faith prior to our cooperating with and trusting them. One need not suppose that because Smith or Jones is not a Christian he therefore has no chance of seeing any important basic truths, or of having a basic decency in him. It does seem to me that sometimes our Evangelical allies mistakenly make the opposite assumptions. And of course those assumptions, it seems to me, also elicit opposite reactions from secularists, who have a real hostility to the Faith, and give some plausibility to their criticisms. This important part of our Catholic heritage should not be lost sight of.

And this is close to the second point mentioned by Hudson which I would like to reiterate. We must insist—again it is part of our great Catholic heritage—that human reason has the capacity to know moral truth. This means, first of all, that some basic, important moral truths are publicly accessible; they do not require extensive learning, expertise, or faith, to be apprehended. Therefore we can and should defend these truths in the public and political arena. The basis of these truths is human nature. Because of the kind of thing they are, because of their nature, human beings are perfected by certain objects or activities, and diminished by other conditions. Thus, all human beings are perfected by life and health, knowledge and aesthetic experience, play and skillful performance, self-integration, friendship, moral goodness itself, religion, and marriage. On the other hand, the diminishing of these objects or activities is objectively bad for human beings: it is true for all human beings that sickness, death, ignorance, broken relationships, and so on are bad and to be avoided or remedied. Choices which respect all of these fundamental human goods, both in ourselves and in all others, are morally right; choices which violate or unduly neglect a basic human good, in ourselves or others, are objectively morally wrong. So, there is an objective standard for ethical questions that we can appeal to in the public and political arena.

My third point concerns a disagreement with Hudson, or if not that, at least a worry about the way he has expressed one of his points. He claims (in his talk) that "ethics presupposes natural theology," that "natural law cannot be affirmed without the affirmation of a lawgiver." Because of this, he says that we should not be so hesitant to speak about God in the public and political arena. To ground human rights properly one must refer to God.

I agree that one cannot affirm a *law* without the notion of a lawgiver. The concept of *law* just is the concept of a directive from a ruler (or rulers) of a community. But I do not agree that one must first know that God exists before one can know (or affirm) any moral truths, including basic human rights. To affirm otherwise is the Divine Command theory, and I

14

believe there are insuperable problems in that position.

On a Divine Command theory an action is right *because* it is commanded by God; being commanded by God is what makes the action right, and in order to know that an action is right one must know (perhaps only implicitly) that it is commanded by God. (So, sometimes it is claimed that one is implicitly aware of God in one's awareness of moral duty—Cardinal Newman, for example, claimed this.) Of course, it is a moral truth that we ought to follow God's commands—holding this does not make one a Divine Command theorist. The Divine Command theorist, however, goes further than this. The Divine Command theorist claims that doing what is right *means* following God's command, or God's will.

The problems with this theory begin when one asks, "Why should I follow God's commands?" This question does not suppose any previous doubt on our part. Rather, while it is true that we certainly ought to follow God's commands, it is an intelligible question, or seems to be, to ask, Why? If this question does have an answer, if one says, "One ought to follow God's commands because"—and then completes the answer in whatever way, then he has given up on the Divine Command theory. If there is a distinct reason why I should follow God's commands, then there is, after all, a ground or reason discoverable independently of God's commands (and distinct from any of God's commands, on pain of being viciously circular) for why I should act thus or so. If one said, for example, that I should follow God's commands because God is wise and we know therefore that his commands will direct me toward what is genuinely fulfilling for me and the good of the universe, then an action's being toward the fulfillment for me and the good of the universe is what makes it right, and not simply that God has willed it. So, to keep to the theory, the Divine Command theorist must refuse to answer the question. He must say that the question does not make sense, that "I should do X," just *means the same as*, "God commands X," and so one cannot intelligibly ask why one should follow God's commands.

While this exchange does not refute the Divine Command theorist, it does clarify his position and suggests the root problem with the theory. For we can now ask the Divine Command theorist: When you say, "I ought to do X means God commands X," what do you mean by "God"? In particular, are you not presupposing that God is *holy* or at least *morally good*? If the Divine Command theorist answers that, no, he is just supposing that God is the omnipotent creator of the universe, then the theory is open to the charge of sheer power worship. Why should we obey the commands of a merely powerful person? One can see prudential reasons to do, but such reasons can scarcely give rise to moral duty. On the other hand, if the Divine Command theorist answers that we should obey God because God is holy, then he points up the fundamental difficulty. Any notion of God that is rich enough so that it makes sense to say we ought to obey God presupposes that we are thinking of God as holy, but that means that we must already have a notion of holiness.

Our notion of God is not innate. We form an analogical concept of God on the basis of perfections and qualities first understood as they exist in creatures. And an important component in our concept of God is holiness—God is not just a powerful master of the universe, but he is holy, supremely morally good. But that means that our concept of God *presupposes* the notion of moral goodness, and so moral goodness cannot just mean following God's will. So, the knowledge of moral truths does not presuppose natural theology.

This is an important point for the context of our political and public discussions. I think it is very important that one can make a point about, say, human rights, or human nature, without presupposing one's whole world-view. As Catholics we do have a rich, inspiring, and true world-view. But not everything we say need presuppose all of it. It seems to me that some Catholics despair of political and public discussions precisely because

16

they think that they cannot establish any valuable point unless they can presuppose the context of the whole Catholic vision. That's a mistake. It is part and parcel of Hegelian idealism, not Christianity, to hold that in order to understand *any*thing you have to understand *every*thing. On the contrary, one can establish certain important truths before one convinces someone to adopt the whole Catholic Christian world-view.

My last comment is not a criticism of Hudson's paper but an addition. I think one reason Catholics have failed to make a political difference in America is that our leaders have often failed to distinguish clearly between differences about means and differences about ends. If we differ with a political candidate about economic measures, usually it is a difference about means. But if a candidate is in favor of abortion, or claims that the government can be neutral on such an issue—which amounts to saying treating unborn human beings as nonpersons is neutrality—this is not a difference about the best way to attain agreed upon ends. It is a difference about ends. We should be clear that there are all sorts of issues on which Catholics can, and will, legitimately disagree. But these should be distinguished from other issues that concern the fundamental moral truths that are non-negotiable. There are some issues on which taking a bad position is more than a disagreement about strategy. Abortion and euthanasia are examples. If a politician does not recognize that it is unjust to give the protection of law to born persons but to deny it to unborn persons, then that politician is either confused or immorally callous about a fundamental issue of justice, and is therefore unfit for public office. Just as we should not endorse Ku Klux Klanners or Nazis, so we should not endorse those who favor abortion.

My last point is simply a hearty agreement with his recommendation of another serious look at Thomistic philosophy. For its acute realism and analytic rigor, it cannot be beat.

PART II

MORAL PLURALISM, PUBLIC REASON AND NATURAL LAW

Moral Pluralism, Public Reason, and Natural Law

Robert P. George
Princeton University
Princeton, New Jersey

Moral Pluralism

Contemporary Anglo-American political philosophy is preoccupied by the problem of moral pluralism. This preoccupation reflects an important social fact about Great Britain, the United States, and other Western nations: People no longer disagree merely about the proper or most effective means of protecting public goods and combatting public evils. People today disagree about what is a public good and what is a public evil. And this disagreement is not merely about what is to count as a *public*, as opposed to a purely *private*, good or evil; it is about what is *morally* good or evil in itself.

Consider, for example, the question of homosexuality. No longer are people divided merely over the question whether the criminalization of sodomy is a proper or effective means of discouraging homosexual conduct. Their disagreement goes beyond the question whether such conduct implicates a legitimate *public* interest justifying legal restriction or is merely a *private* vice which the state has a duty to tolerate. The old consensus about the immorality of homosexual conduct and relationships integrated around such conduct has broken down. Although many people, particularly those who cling to traditional Catholic, Protestant, or Jewish religous faith, continue to believe that homoseuxal acts and relationships are morally bad, many other people, notably including a great many journalists, intellectuals, and other opinion-shaping elites, have adopted the belief that homosexual conduct is no vice at all. "Gay is good," they say. So the debate has shifted from whether or not the state is justified in prohibiting sodomy to the question whether it is justified in refusing to honor homosexual relationships by, for example, declining to issue marriage licenses to same-sex couples.

Disagreement at the moral level also characterizes the issue of abortion. Of course, everyone professes to believe that abortion is, in some sense, a "bad thing." After all, no one would deliberately become pregnant for the pleasure of having an abortion, just as no one would deliberately expose himself to carcinogens for the pleasure of undergoing surgery to remove a malignant tumor. But as to whether abortion is *morally* bad, there is profound disagreement. It is true that a majority of Americans continue to believe that abortion, except in certain rare and exceptional cases (i.e., where pregnancy threatens the life of the mother or would cause her severe and irreparable physical harm, or where it is the result of rape), is indeed morally bad; and something approaching a majority of Americans believe that abortion is a moral evil indistinguishable from infanticide and other forms of homicide. However, a substantial number of Americans support legal abortion and even its public funding for indigent women, not merely on the ground that abortion is a "private" immorality which, as such, the state has a duty to tolerate, but in the belief that abortion is, or can be, a morally good choice.

A similar moral pluralism obtains when it comes to physician-assisted suicide and euthanasia, the recreational use of drugs, and a host of other issues. Some disputed moral issues—particularly, I think, the issue of abortion—bring to mind the moral disagreement over slavery in the United States in the middle third of the nineteenth century. By then, supporters of slavery were no longer content to argue, as they had been in the late-eighteenth century, that the "peculiar institution" was a "necessary evil" whose toleration was required under circumstances in which abolition would produce disastrous, and therefore morally unacceptable, social and economic consequences. Instead, they argued that slavery was morally good and right, and that the position of their abolitionist opponents represented, not a practically unattainable—albeit noble—moral ideal, but, rather, a morally repulsive religious fanaticism. Despite repeated efforts at political compromise, the moral disagreement over slavery proved, in the end, incompatible with peace and social stability. The issue had to be resolved finally by civil war which cost something approaching three-quarters of a million lives.

Reflection on the carnage of the American Civil War inclines me to think that contemporary political theory is right to take seriously the problem of moral pluralism. I am, however, skeptical about philosophical work in this area whose ambitions are to identify basic principles of "political" justice which can be agreed upon by all reasonable people and which promise to provide social stability by constraining the grounds of political advocacy and action when it comes to fundamental moral issues (such as abortion and homosexuality) upon which people today disagree. The most notable—and ambitious—example of philosophical work of this type is the "political liberalism" of John Rawls. In the pages that follow, I shall describe Rawls's effort to identify basic principles of justice which, as the fruit of an "overlapping consensus" among people who otherwise differ over fundamental moral and religious issues, promise to make possible social stability for morally good reasons. Then I shall say why I am skeptical about Rawls's political liberalism. In particular, I shall argue that Rawls's conception of "public reason(s)," i.e., reasons which may legitimately be introduced in political advocacy and acted upon legislatively, is unreasonably narrow and restrictive.

Public Reason and Liberal Legitimacy

In his influential 1971 book *A Theory of Justice*, Rawls defended a liberal conception of justice, which he called "justice as fairness," whose basic principles for a well-ordered society were identified as those that would be chosen by free and equal persons in what he called "the original position." Parties in "the original position" select principles of justice in a state of ignorance regarding their personal moral and religious convictions, social and economic status, and related factors that will distinguish them from many of their fellow citizens when they emerge from behind "the veil of ignorance" to live in a society governed in accordance with the principles they had selected.

In 1993, Rawls published a new book, *Political Liberalism*, which amends certain features of the theory of justice he had advanced in 1971. Most importantly, he now says that the argument for "justice as fairness" as adumbrated in *A Theory of Justice* relied on a premise which was inconsistent with the theory itself, namely, the belief that "in the well-ordered society of justice as fairness, citizens hold the same comprehensive doctrine, and this includes aspects of Kant's comprehensive liberalism, to which the principles of justice as fairness might belong."[1] The problem with this belief is that neither liberalism, considered as what he calls a "comprehensive" (as opposed to a merely "political") doctrine, nor any other comprehensive view (e.g., Catholicism, Judaism, Platonism, Aristotelianism, communism), is held by citizens generally in contemporary pluralistic societies. And a plurality of comprehensive views is, Rawls suggests, natural and unavoidable in the circumstances of political freedom that characterize constitutional democratic regimes. Political theorizing which accepts the legitimacy of such regimes must begin, therefore, by acknowledging what Rawls calls "the fact of reasonable pluralism."

Recognition of "the fact of reasonable pluralism," according to Rawls, rules out the possibility of legitimately defending principles of justice for constitutional democratic regimes by appealing to comprehensive doctrines—including comprehensive forms of liberalism. Some alternative must, therefore, be found. Otherwise, the social stability of such regimes would be in constant jeopardy. Everything would depend on the capacity and willingness of people with fundamentally different moral views— including radically different conceptions of justice and human rights—to reach and preserve a *modus vivendi*. The alternative Rawls proposes is "political liberalism." Its ideal is that "citizens are to conduct their public political discusssions of constitutional essentials and matters of basic justice within the framework of what each sincerely regards as a reasonable political conception of justice, a conception that expresses political values that others as free and equal also might reasonably be expected to endorse."[2]

In such a framework, "deeply opposed though reasonable comprehensive doctrines may live together and all affirm the political conception of a constitutional regime."[3] Where constitutional essentials and matters of basic justice are at issue, public discussion and debate must be conducted—for moral reasons and not as a mere *modus vivendi*—in terms of a "strictly political conception of justice,"[4] and not in terms of moral doctrines of justice associated with the various comprehensive views about which reasonable people disagree. The common affirmation of a "political conception" by adherents of competing comprehensive views enables them to participate in what Rawls refers to as "an overlapping consensus" on basic principles of justice. It is this consensus which makes social stability in the face of moral pluralism not only possible, but possible "for the right reasons."[5]

The nerve of "political liberalism" is the idea that whenever constitutional essentials and matters of basic justice are at stake political actors, including citizens as voters and insofar as they engage in public advocacy of candidates and causes, must refrain from acting on the basis of principles drawn from their comprehensive views (as Kantians, Catholics, communists, or whatever) except to the extent that "public reasons, given by a reasonable political conception, are presented sufficient to support whatever the comprehensive doctrines are introduced to support."[6] Thus, citizens are constrained from appealing to and acting upon beliefs drawn from their most fundamental moral understandings and commitments precisely at the most fundamental political level, viz., the level of constitutional essentials and matters of basic justice. And they are so constrained on grounds entirely separate from the putative falsity, unreasonableness, or unsoundness of those understandings and commitments or the beliefs drawn therefrom.[7]

Rawls insists that "political liberalism is not a form of Enlightenment liberalism, that is, a comprehensive liberal and often secular doctrine founded on reason and suitable for the modern age now that the religious authority of Christian ages is said to be no longer dominant."[8] It is, rather,

> a political conception of political justice for a constitutional democratic regime that a plurality of reasonable doctrines, both religious and nonreligious, liberal and nonliberal, may freely endorse, and so freely live by and come to understand its virtues. Emphatically, it does not aim to replace comprehensive doctrines, religious or nonreligious, but intends to be equally distinct from both and, it hopes, acceptable to both.[9]

"Political liberalism" aspires, then, to be impartial with respect to the viewpoints represented by the various reasonable doctrines which compete for the allegiance of citizens. It "does not attack or criticize any reasonable [comprehensive] view."[10] Rawls says that "rather than confronting religious and nonliberal doctrines with a comprehensive liberal philosophical doctrine, the thought is to formulate a liberal political conception that those nonliberal doctrines might be able to endorse."[11] Hence, the crucial idea of an "overlapping consensus" among comprehensive views which, inasmuch as they accept the fundaments of constitutional democracy, are "reasonable."

So "political liberalism" is a doctrine that is not just for liberals. If Rawls is correct, not only proponents of Kant's or Mill's liberalism, but also faithful Catholics, evangelical Protestants, and observant Jews—assuming the reasonableness of Catholicism, Protestantism, and Judaism (something Rawls suggests he is willing to assume)—ought to be able to join the "overlapping consensus" by reasonably embracing "political liberalism" without compromising their basic religious and moral convictions.[12]

Although Rawls observes that a mere political compromise or *modus vivendi* might, under propitious circumstances, develop into an "overlapping consensus," he carefully distinguishes an "overlapping consensus" from a mere *modus vivendi*. Unlike a *modus vivendi*, an "overlapping consensus" is constituted by a certain level of *moral agreement* about what constitute fair terms of social cooperation among people who, being reasonable, view each other as free and equal citizens. So, although Rawls presents the liberal "political conception" of justice as standing independent of any particular comprehensive doctrine (in that sense it is, he says, a "freestanding" conception), it is nevertheless a *moral* conception, containing "its own intrinsic normative and moral ideal."[13]

Rawls maintains that terms of cooperation offered by citizens to their fellow citizens are fair only insofar as "citizens offering them reasonably think that those citizens to whom such terms are offered might also reasonably accept them."[14] This "criterion of reciprocity" is the core of what Rawls labels "the liberal principle of legitimacy," viz., that "our exercise of political power is fully proper only when it is exercised in accordance with a constitution, the essentials of which all citizens as free and equal may be expected to endorse in the light of principles and ideals acceptable to their common human reason."[15] When, and only when, political power is exercised in accordance with such a constitution do political actors—including voters—maintain fidelity to the ideal of "public reason."

The Challenge of Natural Law Theory

The "liberal principle of legitimacy" and ideal of "public reason" exclude as illegitimate in political discourse and in the exercise of public authority, at least insofar as basic matters of justice—including constitutional rights—are concerned, appeal to principles and propositions drawn from comprehensive doctrines even though they are, or may well be, *true*. It would be one thing to argue that in certain circumstances *prudence* requires such an exclusion, at least temporarily, as part of a *modus vivendi*. It is quite another thing, however, to claim, as Rawls does, that such an exclusion is *morally* required by virtue of "the fact of reasonable pluralism" even in circumstances in which people are not restrained by prudence from acting on principles they reasonably believe to be true, and which are not ruled out as reasons for political action by their reasonable comprehensive doctrines of justice and political morality. So, we must examine the justification Rawls offers for this exclusion. To that end, let us consider what Rawls has in mind in demanding, as a matter of reciprocity, that citizens offer to their fellow citizens with whom they disagree about basic moral, metaphysical, and religious matters terms of social cooperation which they reasonably think their fellow citizens may reasonably accept.

If Rawls's "criterion of reciprocity" and "liberal principle of legitimacy" are interpreted narrowly, then citizens offering terms of cooperation to their fellow citizens who happen to disagree with them about a matter in dispute must merely think that they are presenting to their fellow citizens sound reasons, accessible to them as reasonable people of goodwill, for changing their minds. The scope of "public reason" under this narrow interpretation of reciprocity and legitimacy would be wide. It would, to be sure, rule out as illegitimate claims based on the allegedly "secret knowledge" of a gnostic elite or the putative truths revealed only to a select few and not accessible to reasonable persons as such, but it would not exclude any principle or proposition, however controversial, that is put forward for acceptance on the basis of rational argumentation.

Now, even on this narrow interpretation, some religious believers would object that their views would be unfairly excluded from public political discourse. Others, however, would have no objection to a principle of reciprocity which demands only that they offer "public reasons" in this very wide sense. They would have no interest in restraining the liberty of their fellow citizens, or in disfavoring them or their preferred ways of life or modes of behavior, on the basis of claims they could not defend by rational argumentation. They would accept the claim that to do so would be unfair. It seems clear, however, that Rawls himself cannot accept the narrow interpretation of reciprocity and the correspondingly very wide conception of public reason. His goal, after all, is to limit the range of morally acceptable doctrines of political morality in circumstances of moral pluralism to a single doctrine: viz., "political liberalism." The very wide conception of public reason simply will not accomplish that goal. It will not, for example, rule out appeals to principles and propositions drawn from comprehensive forms of liberalism. More importantly, it will not exclude appeals to principles and propositions drawn from nonliberal comprehensive doctrines which content themselves with appeals to "our common human reason."

Notable among such doctrines is the broad tradition of

natural law thinking about morality, justice, and human rights. This tradition poses an especially interesting problem for Rawls's theory of public reason because of its integration into Roman Catholic teaching. So it is, at once, a nonliberal comprehensive philosophical doctrine *and* part of a larger religious tradition which, in effect, proposes its own principle of public reason, viz., that questions of law and policy (including what Rawls has in mind when he refers to "constitutional essentials and matters of basic justice") ought to be decided in accordance with natural law, natural rights, and/or natural justice (where, as in Aquinas's natural law theory, something is good, or right or just "by nature" insofar as it is *reasonable*).[16]

If Rawls is to successfully defend a conception of "public reason" narrow enough to exclude appeals to natural law theory, he must show that there is something unfair about such appeals. And he must, of course, demonstrate this unfairness without appeal to comprehensive liberalism or any other comprehensive conception of justice which competes with the natural law conception. In other words, he must avoid smuggling into the defense of his claim that "*only* a political conception of justice ... can serve as a basis of public reason and justification"[17] principles or propositions which are themselves in dispute among adherents to reasonable comprehensive doctrines (including, of course, Catholicism and natural law theory). This, it seems to me, he has not done and, I believe, cannot do.

Rawls does not explicitly address the claims of natural law theorists—Catholic or otherwise. He seems, however, to have somthing like their beliefs in mind in his critique of what he calls "rationalist believers who contend that [their] beliefs are open to and can be fully established by reason."[18] Rawls's argument against the so-called "rationalist believers" rests entirely on the claim that they unreasonably deny "the fact of reasonable pluralism." But do they? I am myself something of a "rationalist believer," at least according to Rawls's definition, and I certainly do not deny the fact that people in our culture, including reasonable people, disagree about fundamental moral questions, including questions pertaining to homosexuality, abortion, physician-assisted suicide, and the recreational use of drugs. Nor do I deny that some measure of moral disagreement—though not necessarily moral disagreement on the scale of what we find today in the United States, for example—is inevitable under circumstances of political and religious liberty. So I do not see how Rawls can justify his claim that "rationalist believers" deny "the fact of reasonable pluralism."

Rawls own methodological and moral commitments require him to avoid denying the soundness, reasonableness, or truth of the reasonable, if controversial, moral, metaphysical, and religious claims that his "political" conception of justice would exclude from political discourse and as grounds for political action. So he cannot rule out the views of natural law theorists or "rationalist believers" on issues such as homosexuality, abortion, euthanasia, and drugs on the grounds that their views are unsound, unreasonable, or false. If he is reduced to arguing for the unsoundness, unreasonableness, or falsity of these views, then his "*political* liberalism" will have collapsed into "*comprehensive* liberalism." And we are left with the conflict of comprehensive views to which "political liberalism" is meant to provide an alternative.

Understandably, then, Rawls seeks to avoid engaging the specific claims and arguments of the "rationalist believers." He limits himself to a simple denial that their claims "can be publicly and fully established by reason."[19] But how can this denial be sustained independently of some engagement "on the merits" with the specific arguments they advance in their public political advocacy—arguments which Rawls's idea of "public reason" is meant to exclude in advance without the need to address their soundness and reasonableness or the truth or falsity of the principles and propositions in support of which they are offered?

It will not do for Rawls to claim that he is not denying the truth of a "rationalist believer's" claims but merely their assertion that these claims can be publicly and fully established by reason. What makes a "rationalist believer" a "rationalist" is precisely his belief that his principles can be justified by *rational argument* and his willingness to provide just such *rational argumentation*. The arguments he offers by way of justifying his principles and their applications to specific political issues will either be sound or unsound. If they are sound, then Rawls can give no reason for excluding the principles they vindicate on the ground that they are illegitimate reasons for political action; if they are unsound, then they ought to be rejected precisely on that basis, and not because the principles in support of which they are offered are, in Rawls's sense, "nonpublic."

Let us return, though, to Rawls's claim that "rationalist believers" deny "the fact of reasonable pluralism." He states that "[i]t is unrealistic—or worse, it arouses mutual suspicion and hostility—to suppose that all our differences are rooted in ignorance and perversity, or else in the rivalries for power, status, and economic gain."[20] Natural law theorists and (other?) "rationalist believers" do not deny this. Indeed, they recognize that differences of opinion and commitment often arise from factors which reason does not control—matters of taste and sentiment, for example. Moreover, matters can sometimes be rationally underdetermined even where reason guides reflection by excluding as unreasonable certain possibilities, but leaving more than one possibility open and, in that sense, rationally available. On some issues, there are a variety of unreasonable opinions, but no uniquely reasonable or correct one.

Natural law theorists (and others) maintain, however, that on certain other issues, including certain fundamental moral and political issues, there are uniquely correct answers. The question whether there is a human right against being enslaved, for example, or being punished for one's religious beliefs, admits of a uniquely correct answer which is available in principle to every rational person. Pro-life advocates assert that there is similarly a human right against deliberate feticide and other forms of direct killing of innocent persons. Differences over such issues as slavery, religious freedom, abortion, and euthanasia may be "reasonable" in the sense that reasonable persons can err in their judgments and arrive at morally incorrect positions. But, assuming there is a truth of these matters—something Rawls cannot deny and, one would think, has no desire to deny—errors of reason must be responsible for anyone's failure to arrive at the morally correct positions. There are many possible roots of such errors, not all of which involve cuplability or subjective guilt on the part of individuals who make them. Ignorance of, or inattention to, certain relevant facts or values may be the source of a particular error. Prejudice or other subrational influences—which may be pervasive in a culture or subculture making it difficult for any of its individual members to reason well about certain issues—may block insights which are critical to sound moral judgments. And, of course, logical failures or other errors in the reasoning process can deflect judgment in the moral field as they can in all other fields of inquiry. Nothing in the position of natural law theorists (or "rationalist believers") entails the proposition that we can always easily arrive at correct moral positions or that we will not sometimes (perhaps often) get things wrong.

Is anything in their view *unreasonable*? Rawls certainly cannot declare their view unreasonable because they maintain that on certain morally-charged and highly disputed political questions—including questions of human rights—there are uniquely morally correct answers. The fact that "reasonable people" can be found on competing sides of such questions in no way implies that the competing views are equally reasonable. Reasonable people can be wrong—as Rawls himself implicitly acknowledges in his claims against the "rationalist believers" who are, after all, reasonable people even if their claim that their beliefs can be fully and publicly justified by reason is unreasonable. There is simply no unreasonableness in maintaining that otherwise reasonable people can be less than fully reasonable (sometimes cuplably, other times not) in their judgments of particular issues.[21]

In *A Theory of Justice*, Rawls identified the two basic principles of "justice as fairness" by the method of "political constructivism" which asked what substantive principles would be chosen by parties in the "original position" behind the "veil of ignorance" which hides from them (among other things) what Rawls now calls their "comprehensive views." In a key passage of *Political Liberalism*, he says that the "liberal principle of legitimacy" and the ideal of "public reason" have "the same basis as the substantive principles of justice."[22] It seems to me, however, that this basis was, and remains, insecure. Over more than twenty-five years, Rawls and his followers have failed to provide any reason to suppose that "perfectionist" principles— principles of justice or political morality more generally drawn from "comprehensive views" about what is humanly valuable and morally upright—which would not be selected under conditions of artificial ignorance by the unnaturally risk-averse parties in the "original position" are *unjust* (or cannot be valid principles or justice). Rawlsians seem to suppose that from the proposition that principles which would be selected *by such parties under such conditions* are just (i.e., involve no injustice), it follows that perfectionist principles—which might very well be chosen by reasonable and well-informed persons outside the original position—are unjust. *Non sequitur.*

1. John Rawls, *Political Liberalism*, paperback edition (New York: Columbia University Press, 1996), p. xlii.

2. Rawls, *Political Liberalism*, p. 1.

3. Rawls, *Political Liberalism*, p. xx.

4. Rawls, *Political Liberalism*, p. xvii.

5. Rawls, *Political Liberalism*, pp. xlii, 388, 390, and 392. Rawls's emphasis on the need for social stability in the face of moral pluralism should not lead the reader to suppose that his argument for "political liberalism" is merely pragmatic. A "strictly political" conception of justice is, he maintains, the *fairest* and *most reasonable* way of resolving questions of constitutional essentials and matters of basic justice.

6. Rawls introduces this "wide view" of public reason in the Introduction to the Paperback Edition of *Political Liberalism*, p. lii. It represents a broadening of the more restrictive view set forth in the text, pp. 247-252.

7. Rawls says that appeals to comprehensive doctrines are never legitimate in legislative assemblies or in the public acts and pronouncements of executives officers. Nor may judges in interpreting the Constitution or justifying their interpretations rely upon or invoke principles drawn from comprehensive doctrines. See *Political Liberalism*, p. 215.

8. Rawls, *Political Liberalism*, p. xl.

9. Rawls, *Political Liberalism*, p. xl.

10. Rawls, *Political Liberalism*, p. xxi.

11. Rawls, *Political Liberalism*, p. xxi.

12. In what has become a famous footnote in *Political Liberalism*, Rawls defends what he describes as a "duly qualified" right to abortion in the first trimester (and possibly beyond). See n. 32, pp. 243-244. He treats the matter as a falling within the category of constitutional essentials and matters of basic justice to which his doctrine of "public reason" applies, concluding that "we would go against the ideal of public reason if we voted from a comprehensive doctrine that denied this right." This by itself should raise doubts in the minds of serious Catholics, Protestants, and Jews who consider whether their views have a place in Rawls's "overlapping consensus."

13. Rawls, *Political Liberalism*, p. xliv.

14. Rawls, *Political Liberalism*, p. xliv.

15. Rawls, *Political Liberalism*, p. 137.

16. See St. Thomas Aquinas, *Summa theologiae*, I-II, q. 71, a. 2c: "The good of the human being is in accord with reason, and human evil is being outside the order of reasonableness." On the proper interpretation of Aquinas on this point, see John Finnis, *Natural Law and Natural Rights* (Oxford: Clarendon Press, 1980), p. 36. See also Finnis's more detailed account in *Aquinas* (Oxford: Oxford University Press, 1998).

17. Rawls, *Political Liberalism*, p. 137 (emphasis supplied).

18. Rawls, *Political Liberalism*, pp. 152-153.

19. Rawls, *Political Liberalism*, p. 153.

20. Rawls, *Political Liberalism*, p. 153.

21. In fairness to Rawls, I should aknowledge here his treatment of the sources of moral disagreement in connection with what he calls "the burdens of judgment." *Political*

Liberalism, p. 58. However, to preserve the integrity of his political liberalism, we must read his account of the sources of disagreement in such a way as to avoid its collapse into relativism. If we do, then Rawls's idea of "fully reasonable," and even "perfectly reasonable," though erroneous, views refers to false beliefs which are formed without subjective fault. I think that this is what people generally have in mind when, though fully persuaded of the truth of a certain view, they allow nevertheless that "reasonable people" can disagree with them. The fact of "reasonable disagreement" in this sense is certainly not a valid warrant for ruling out argument as to the truth of matters in dispute on the ground that reasons adduced in any argument "on the merits" cannot qualify as "public reasons."

22.   Rawls, *Political Liberalism*, p. 225.

Rawls, Liberalism, and the Unity of Reason

David M. Gallagher
The Catholic University of America
Washington, D.C.

In response to Professor George's paper, I would like to make four points.

I. In Defense of Rawls

Professor George has asked what justification Rawls can give for excluding from political discussions appeals to comprehensive doctrines in general and specifically a doctrine of natural law. I think Rawls would respond to Professor George in two ways.

First he would say that an appeal to natural law of the sort George proposes, while possible, is simply unnecessary for political life. Rawls begins with the fact of pluralism among comprehensive doctrines; the overlapping consensus is precisely the *agreement* that people with differing comprehensive doctrines can and should have with regard to fundamental political matters. A person's affirmation of what falls within the consensus is a part of his larger comprehensive doctrine, and, for that person, could be justified on the basis of principles found in that larger doctrine. Thus each person would give a justification for the political view he shares with others, but would do so from the distinct point of view of his comprehensive doctrine.[1] For example, a Catholic, a Kantian, and a Utilitarian may all agree in rejecting slavery as a political possibility; their rationale for this rejection, however, when based on their comprehensive doctrines, would not be the same. Rawls' position is that we can all argue for something like the rejection of slavery on the basis of a properly political reasoning (i.e. limited to political questions) which we can all share and which is autonomous, i.e. independent of any larger metaphysical or comprehensive view of things.[2] It is precisely this shared "public reasoning," the kind of reasoning required for a pluralistic society, that he is attempting to develop and justify. Given this shared basis it is not necessary to argue on the basis of a comprehensive doctrine such as natural law.

Second, Rawls would say that it is morally wrong to do so. Here Rawls might say something like the following. "You are indeed right to say that a natural law doctrine can justify political views and, moreover, a person who accepts the larger view of natural law (e.g. a Catholic) should, for himself or for those who agree with him, so employ that doctrine. What is more, such a person may be absolutely right or true in so justifying his views and even uniquely so. Nevertheless, when that person in a pluralistic society enters into political discussions with others who do not accept the natural law doctrine, then he should refrain from using natural law arguments. He should so refrain, not merely because it is ineffective to use an argument with someone who does not accept its premises, but also—and this is morally significant—because such an argument does not really respect the other as an equal, rational participant in the democratic process.[3] To use an argument you know is based on premises another does not accept constitutes a lack of respect; it is as though you wanted to move the person to act a certain way without giving him any reasons; i.e., reasons he can see as reasons." So, to employ such arguments in that context would be, practically speaking, not to acknowledge a very fundamental truth: the persons taking part in the discussion are rational agents and should be appealed to and moved on the basis of rational arguments.[4]

II. The Unity and Disunity of Reason

I believe that the real issue dividing Professor George and Rawls has to do with their respective notions of what I will call the "unity of reason". To see this it is necessary to summarize briefly how Professor George disagrees with Rawls, especially with regard to the second response of Rawls. The argument goes as follows. If someone holds a comprehensive doctrine and does so for reasons which are available to all (e.g., the "rational believer" whose beliefs are based on rational proof), then it does not seem that he would offend anyone in espousing and appealing to that doctrine in public debates, especially if he gives for that doctrine those reasons that are publicly available. The "rational believer" does in fact respect all the other participants in the discussion because he does indeed give reasons that the others can accept. *De facto*, not all other persons may accept his reasons, but the important thing is that those others could, in principle, see the cogency of such arguments and consequently accept a political view they support. In other words, for a person who believes that natural law is a doctrine available to any rational being, to justify a political position on the basis of natural law constitutes no lack of respect for one's fellow citizens taken as rational agents. There is nothing *unreasonable* about arguing in this fashion. Natural law reasoning would, in fact, be public reasoning.

Now, if Prof. George's argument is so simply and clear, and I think it is, why would Rawls resist it? This question brings to light a certain presupposition of Rawls, a basic presupposition that underlies his whole system. I call this presupposition the "Disunity of Reason." When Professor George speaks of holding a comprehensive doctrine such as natural law on the basis of reasons available to all rational persons, he is presupposing, first, that reason as such tends toward the truth, so that apart from obstructing influences (there are many) reason will affirm the truth when it is apparent. Second, he is presupposing that the reasons or minds of all rational beings are more or less alike. That is to say, in arriving at the truth, all rational beings arrive at the same truth. Hence, if I have cogent arguments for some view and I get you to see those cogent arguments, then you too will affirm that view (unless there is some obstructing factor). This is what I would call the "Unity of Reason". On this view, reason, as found in all individuals, naturally tends toward a unitary set of truths.

In my opinion, Rawls ultimately rejects the unity of reason. This appears most clearly in his oft repeated statement to the effect that pluralism in comprehensive doctrines is not merely a fact that characterizes our times, but is rather the natural result of reason when it is left to work on its own in the context of free institutions. If reason is not held in check by the use of political force (e.g., religious persecution, censorship, government control of the universities and media), then the natural—and, for Rawls, desirable—consequence is that a plurality of mutually inconsistent comprehensive doctrines will arise.[5] That is to say that such pluralism is the result of reason left to operate naturally. Reason naturally tends not to unity but to disunity. Of course Rawls does not mean that each individual has a distinct comprehensive doctrine; there will be many long-lasting and fairly stable traditions to one or the other of which most people will belong.[6] Nevertheless, it is plurality and not unity to which reason naturally tends.

At the same time, Rawls is not a skeptic or a complete relativist. He does hold that truth is possible, and that if two views are contradictory or in opposition both cannot be true. It may well be that one comprehensive view is true and all the others false. Of course, not embracing skepticism or relativism is important for Rawls, since relativism, in calling into question all values, would call into question the very political values that he wants so much to affirm.[7] How then could it be that truth exists, but that reason naturally misses it for the most part? It must be that reason itself accounts for this situation. It must be, to use a simple analogy, that the several reasons are like mirrors, all slightly differently curved. Thus, while there is a single, true reality which is reflected, the way it looks when reflected will differ from mirror to mirror. So too, our individual reasons are such that they do not naturally all affirm the same things to be true, even though there may be a single truth.[8]

This natural disunity implies that I cannot expect that other persons who see things differently from me can be brought to see things as I do. Their reason is such that they see things as they do, and my reason is such that I see things as I do. If I try to convince them to see things a certain way based on the way that I see things, I obviously will fail. Only if our minds were alike would my reasons be cogent reasons for them. Thus for Rawls, the naturalness of pluralism precludes a unification; what is more, it means that I have to expect that others will not be able to understand my reasonings, that I will not be able to convince them based on the way I see things, that what count as cogent reasons for me will not be cogent reasons for them. Obviously, this sort of understanding of reason renders any meaningful debate at the level of comprehensive doctrines impossible. And this, I think is Rawl's view (although he does not spell out the disunity so explicitly). He simply would not accept Professor George's assumption that there can be reasons, at the level of comprehensive doctrines, that would be cogent for all. This is what he means when he says that it is unreasonable to deny the fact of reasonable pluralism: it is unreasonable to act as if people could accept your reasons.[9]

Thus if we accept the unity of reason, George would seem to be right; it is possible to have reasons for a comprehensive view that are potentially reasons for everyone, and so it should be legitimate to employ such reasons, even in political discourse. If we accept the disunity, however, George is not right; his assumption that there could be reasons for comprehensive doctrines available to all is simply not correct; even if I happen to think my reasons are reasons for all, I should recognize that others will not (and probably cannot) agree with me. And so to use such reasons would be a lack of respect for them as autonomous, free participants in public life.

III. The Legitimate Role of Liberalism

For Rawls, as for many nowadays, liberalism is *in principle* the only adequate form of political rule. The reason for this has to do with liberalism's relation to pluralism. Liberalism, as a doctrine (if it can be called a doctrine), holds that civil government should not be officially bound to any particular comprehensive doctrine—especially any religious doctrine—but should leave all such matters to the individuals. That is to say, it does not officially take any stand on what Yves Simon referred to as "transcendent truths"; it claims to be neutral with respect to the various answers that are given to the questions of ultimate origins and ultimate destiny.[10] Such a liberal government does not pretend to foster or hinder any particular view, nor does it claim to justify its policies in terms of any such view; in a liberal society ultimate beliefs are private matters and individuals are allowed maximum liberty to act on their beliefs.

Historically the rise of the liberal approach to political rule has seemed to follow upon the introduction of a pluralism among ultimate, religious beliefs. If the people in society do not share beliefs about ultimate matters, then the government, which deals with common matters, should not attempt to get involved in these questions. If government does get involved, it will necessarily take one view or another and will end up imposing that view on those who disagree with it, and, being government, will do so with force. This is to do violence to its own citizens. Anyone who proposes a non-liberal regime convicts himself, *ipso facto*, of a desire to impose his own ultimate views unfairly on others who do not share them. Thus for someone like Rawls, for whom pluralism among comprehensive doctrines is the natural state of affairs, a liberal approach to government is the only adequate approach.

What should we say about the status of liberalism if we reject Rawls' assumption of a disunity in reason? If we accept a unity of reason, then we must also accept the existence of ultimate truths the same for all. Should we then simply reject liberalism as a sort of social indifference to these most important truths? In perhaps oversimplified terms, is liberalism—public neutrality on transcendent questions—a bad thing?

The answer to this question is not simple. In one sense liberalism is not a good thing at all. If liberalism is introduced to deal with situations of pluralism, then we should have to say that it implies a bad situation. For anyone who believes in the unity of reason, pluralism at the highest level (i.e., with respect to the ultimate questions) is a decidedly bad thing. If there are five competing views, at least four must be false. And if the general population is more or less evenly distributed among these five views, then most of the people suffer under mistaken notions about themselves, the universe and God. This is not a good thing. So, if liberalism implies pluralism and pluralism is bad, then liberalism would seem not to be a good thing. It is like eyeglasses; if a person has to wear eyeglasses, that is not a good thing, for it means that his eyes are not as they should be.

But then again, for a person whose eyes are not good, eyeglasses seem to be, in a way, a rather good thing, for the person is better off with the glasses than without them. Glasses are a good solution for a bad situation. So too it would seem for liberalism, if we do accept the unity of reason. It would be better, all things considered, to have unanimity among the body politic on the ultimate questions, and if there were such agreement, a number of matters consequent upon the shared comprehensive doctrine could enter into political life. Public life would be richer, would produce more good for its citizens, if it included aspects of the transcendent. But if there is not unanimity, if there is factual plurality, then it seems that the liberal approach is needed: if we cannot agree on ultimate matters, let us, instead of constantly fighting about them, make them private and keep for the public domain only those things we can agree upon, things like security from criminals and from foreign powers. Liberalism is like eyeglasses, a good remedy for a defective situation. Nevertheless, it does not remedy all the evils of the situation, nor, like eyeglasses, does it provide a cure.

The point here is that when we accept the unity of reason, then it seems a mistake to take the liberal approach to political life as *in principle* the best or the only adequate one. It may be best here and now, but only because we are in a defective situation, that of widespread error concerning ultimate questions. But we should not think that because we need a liberal government in our particular historical circumstances, that it should be imposed always and everywhere. For example, a homogeneous Christian or even Catholic society could justifiably enact "illiberal" policies proscribing things like divorce and pornography or prescribing something like specifically Christian religious education in state schools. At the same time, if we do live in circumstances that require liberal government, then we should be prepared to work in that context and not to be surprised at the evils that it both allows and, at times, promotes.

IV. Natural Law and Public Reason

What difference does it make for our participation in public debate whether we accept or deny the unity of reason? As we have seen, if we accept Rawls' view about the disunity of reason, then he would seem to be right when he concludes that in public discourse a person should neither argue on the basis of his own comprehensive view, a view not shared by all, nor try to use government policy to introduce into the public realm prescriptions or proscriptions based on his own comprehensive doctrines. He should "respect" the beliefs of the others in society and allow the others to pursue them. This is not an unfamiliar refrain; Catholics (or The Moral Majority) are reprehensible when they try to "impose" on everyone, values they accept as part of their own comprehensive religious belief but which others reject. As Mario Cuomo stated in his famous Notre Dame speech: "The values derived from religious belief will not—*and should not*—be accepted as part of the public morality unless they are shared by the pluralistic community at large, by consensus" (emphasis added).[11]

But if we accept, as Professor George rightly does, the unity of reason, the matter is otherwise. If I am convinced that my comprehensive doctrine is true and is true for all even if they do not admit that, then it does not seem that I can responsibly refrain from introducing that view and its practical consequences into public discussion. Of course, how and when I do so will be a question of prudence, a question of suitability to present circumstances, but *in principle*, I will try to have my view be incorporated into the governing view. For example, if I think that God alone is Lord of life and death, and that it does not fall to any human being to decide when a person, including himself, should die (leave off the death penalty here), then I will consider assisted suicide a grave injustice on the part of all concerned. And if I also think it a task of the civil authorities to prevent grave injustices, then I will think it a good thing for assisted suicide to be outlawed. I take it to be true that it will be better for our society to have such a law. Of course I know that people disagree with me, but the mere fact of disagreement does not alter my conviction. I must necessarily see those who disagree with me as being in error; I am, in a way, like a mother who insists what her child put on a coat before going outside on a cold day. I know better what is good for them than they themselves do. And so, if I am convinced that this is better for the whole society, and if I, as a good citizen, want what is best for my society, then I shall have to work to have my views incorporated into public life.

Here, specifically, the issue of natural law that Professor George has raised is important. The moral issues debated in our times are not matters of confessional faith—no one is proposing the prescription or the proscription of infant baptism or of the Mass—but rather issues common to all human beings, issues ultimately that are to be determined according to the natural law. And so it seems perfectly legitimate and reasonable that a person should argue for public policies in these areas on the basis of natural law. As Jacques Maritain pointed out, natural law is common to all rational human beings; in this regard it has an advantage over any appeals to specific religious beliefs. On the basis of natural law there is not only a possibility and indeed likelihood of agreeing with others on moral issues, but in addition there is a basis for rational discussion when there is disagreement, and ultimately the possibility of bringing a person to accept a truth in practical matters which he earlier rejected.[12]

Finally, it is it worth making the obvious remark that the point of debate on public matters is to convince people to accept a view they did not previously accept. If this were not the case, we would simply vote without discussion. This means, however, that debate over public issues is not simply an attempt to get others to act a certain way, but also an occasion—an opportunity—to bring others to the truth I possess and they lack. That is to say, public debate is an occasion of teaching. And here we might return to the question of respecting those who do not agree with us, those who might have a different comprehensive doctrine. Public debate is an occasion for teaching others, not only about immediate practical questions, but also about more fundamental principles, the sort that are included in what Rawls' calls "comprehensive doctrines." It seems to me, in the end, a far higher degree of respect for others as rational beings to make the attempt to convince them of the truth than to abandon them to their "reasonable" error.

Notes

1. John Rawls, *Political Liberalism* (New York: Columbia University Press, 1993), pp. 12, 126-29.

2. Rawls, pp. 9-13, 40.

3. Rawls, p. 137.

4. Rawls, pp. 216-18; cf. pp. 35, 62, 226.

5. Rawls, pp. xxiv-xxv, 36-37, 135, 144, 150, 216-17.

6. Rawls, p. 59.

7. Rawls, pp. 150-54.

8. Given that individuals are usually grouped into larger traditions, the analogy would actually be more like groups of mirrors all like one another, such that you can talk within the group but not outside the group.

9. Rawls, pp. 61, 153.

10. *A General Theory of Authority* (Notre Dame: The University of Notre Dame Press, 1980), p. 108.

11. "Religious Belief and Public Morality: A Catholic Governor's Perspective," in *More than Words: The Speeches of Mario Cuomo*, (New York: St. Martin's Press, 1993), pp. 38-39.

12. See e.g., *Man and the State* (Chicago: the University of Chicago Press, 1951), pp. 76-94.

PART III

BUILDING THE CULTURE OF LIFE IN THE CITY

The *Gospel of Life* in the City

Rev. Stephen F. Brett, SSJ
St. Charles Borromeo Seminary
Philadelphia, Pennsylvania

It has been said that the march of civilization is slow because so many are out of step. Perhaps no other human reality is so out of step with the *Gospel of Life* today as the city. That this should happen is not news for a faith built upon a tradition that looks warmly but warily at bright lights and big cities. Life in the big city has rarely run the risk of being confused with the *City of God* sketched imaginatively by Augustine while the Roman Empire was disintegrating. Jesus wept over the city of Jerusalem (Luke 19.41) and the apostle Paul describes in detail the perils of living in Corinth and Damascus (2 Cor 11.26-33). At the same time great cultural centers have often come into existence through talent and genius, so we are not here to organize a retreat into a contemporary *Walden Pond.* Our task is to find the good news of Christ in the culture of the city and to make the culture of Christ the good news of the city.

In the nineteenth century Soren Kierkegaard subjected the concept of "Christendom" to a withering critique. He believed that this benign term camouflaged the reality of paganism:

> When one sees what it is to be a Christian in Denmark, how could it occur to anyone that this is what Jesus Christ talks about: cross and agony and suffering,

crucifying the flesh, suffering for the doctrine, being salt, being sacrificed, etc.?[1]

There is no longer any cover for Christians. Whatever artificial supports that may have existed to buttress religious expression are disappearing. Expressions of faith, insofar as they can be found, tend to be prophetic, not pharisaic. We do indeed confront agony and suffering in our cities but in a diabolical counterfeit of the suffering of Christ: death through drugs and gang violence; the disappearance of the father from the family, the entangling patterns of dependency that deprive the human spirit of a chance to grow and give.

As the pastor of an inner-city church for two years, I have witnessed the acute struggle of countless individuals to find God in a setting that jeopardizes faith instead of reinforcing it. But the statistics on the unheavenly city, all too real and verifiable, do not diminish the reality of God's love. Urban entropy must always yield to divine energy. I discovered that all, even nonbelievers, esteemed the church as a real instance, perhaps the only one for many, of divine mercy. In the church, God's home, all could be at home, finding forgiveness and family in the embrace of the Eucharist.

When we reflect upon the historical reality that Jesus wept over Jerusalem (and of course Kierkegaard over Copenhagen) we can part company from the bleakness of Kierkegaard's sentiments, drawing strength from the abiding character of the virtue of hope, precisely because of the mysterious power of Christ's cross. Consider the insight of a scholar who knew well the life of Christ in cultures and cities. In his work *The Historical Reality of Christian Culture*, Christopher Dawson wrote:

Even a Christian minority, which lives a hidden and persecuted life, like the early Christians in the ages of the catacombs, possesses its own patterns of life and thought, which are the seeds of a new culture.[2]

We are pleased this morning to have two distinguished speakers who will reflect with us on the reality of a culture in confusion but not without hope. While we have here no lasting city (Heb 13.14) we share the Gospel of Christ, ever ancient and ever new, illuminating hearts and streets poised to encounter the Risen Lord.

Notes

1. Soren Kierkegaard, *Attack upon "Christendom,"* translated by Walter Lowrie (Princeton: Princeton University Press, 1944), p. 97.

2. Christopher Dawson, *The Historical Reality of Christian Culture* (New York: Harper & Brothers, 1960), p. 68.

To Heal Spiritual Alienation

Gerald L. Campbell
The Impact Group, Inc.
Alexandria, Virginia

With the collapse of the Soviet Union and its East European empire, the United States has become the undisputed economic, military, political, and cultural power in the world. Abroad, America inspires a commitment to economic progress, individual freedom, democratic values, and peace that is shared in varying degrees by nearly all the peoples and nations of the world. At home, America's economy continues to be an engine of opportunity and her technological inventiveness keeps on igniting dreams for countless dreamers. Clearly, the United States stands poised for a new and dynamic 'golden age' full of opportunity, prosperity, and peace.

Institutional and Moral Breakdown or A Crisis of the Spirit?

Nevertheless, the long-term prospects for a bright and auspicious future in America are far from guaranteed. Dramatic changes in society are already threatening our way of life. Over the past four decades, the U.S. has become the world's leader in most categories of social pathology. Violent crime has increased sixfold since 1960. Over one hundred thousand Americans have been murdered in the U.S. since 1990—almost twice the number killed in the Vietnam War. Thirty-five percent of all births in the U.S. are illegitimate and nearly half of all marriages end in divorce. The chance that a child in America will live with both parents until age eighteen is now less than thirty percent. Even suicide rates among teenagers have tripled since 1960. Suicide now ranks as the leading cause of teenage death and for every teenage suicide there are fifty to one hundred suicide attempts that have failed.

Our schools reflect this social turbulence. In 1940, America's teachers were asked to identify the major problems in public schools. They replied: chewing gum, making noise, talking out of turn, running in halls, cutting in line, dress code infractions, and littering. In 1990, the answer was: drug and alcohol abuse, pregnancy, suicide, rape, robbery, and assault.

This empirical sketch is disturbing. And yet, there are profound spiritual trends in our lives that should cause even greater concern. Reflect for a moment. Try to visualize how the dynamics of spiritual alienation have been shaping American society. Personal relationships—whether within a family, among friends, at work, or with strangers—have become increasingly self-centered. The family today resembles more a collection of detached individuals than a community of love. Democratic atomism is on the rise. The nation's legal system has become excessively, and even ritualistically, litigious. Our national language has become disturbingly shrill, self-righteous, and judgmental. Too many Americans feel abandoned and alone. Competition has taken precedence over cooperation. Bureaucratic control has triumphed over genuine human interaction in both the public and private sectors.

Even more profoundly, there exists deep within the American consciousness an existential apprehension about the aimless and self-destructive fragmentation that characterizes so much of our social, economic, legal, political, educational, cultural, and even religious life. Try as one might, the simple, but unyielding truth is that no individual today can escape the ubiquitous impact of cynicism and distrust, violence and fear, intemperance and injustice, isolation and aloneness, spiritual emptiness and, most disturbing of all, the absence of mercy. Clearly, there is a profound 'spiritual restlessness' across the land and the quiet voices of the soul are beginning to 'cry out' in rebellion against the dehumanizing structures and alienating dynamics of daily life.

This drama—which is truly a tragedy of American individualism—carries with it great dangers. For if the spiritual forces of alienation are allowed to gain ascendency over the spiritual forces of community—and if they are able to generate a profound and uncontrollable fear of all others by each member of society—a repressive political regime will slowly emerge as a practical necessity to protect freedom. Free individuals—acting from fear—will rush to embrace this regime as the most practical means of securing their person and property. To be sure, many would resist. But, resistance itself would occasion further discord and the need for more control.

Already, the 'fear of others' has begun to seep into the American character. The freedom to go where you want, the freedom to associate with whom you care, the freedom to say what you believe, and the freedom to be free of fear have all been marginalized? Indeed, if anyone were to analyze ordinary human relationships today they would detect the contaminating influence of distrust and fear.

Let's not forget: freedom depends upon the quality of relationships that individuals have with one another. Wherever spiritual alienation exists, freedom has already been diminished!

And so, it is not unreasonable to conclude from these existential dynamics: 1) that spiritual alienation is the underlying cause of an entire range of anti-social behavior, including homelessness, welfare dependency, substance abuse, criminal violence, gang activity, and racial hostility; 2) that spiritual alienation cuts across every social and economic category, and that it affects the quality of life for all Americans, even those who are seemingly outside its influence; 3) that spiritual alienation accounts for the increasingly dysfunctional nature of our most fundamental institutions, including all social, economic, legal, political, educational, and religious institutions as well as the family itself; and 4) that spiritual alienation fragments the essential fabric of civilized society, including our national language, and that it has been a major force in introducing a reckless arbitrariness into our understanding of the nature of man, the family, the individual, community, and even human freedom itself.

Spiritual Alienation:
A Domestic and National Security Crisis

My interest in exploring the spiritual dynamics of love and alienation as the underlying cause of all social dysfunctions grew directly out of insights developed during my six years as Senior Advisor to the Director of the United States Information Agency. During that period, I had many occasions to speak with foreign visitors who had come to America under the auspices of the Agency's Office of Private Sector Programs and Office of International Visitors. What I found most surprising about these discussions was that these visitors expressed a strong desire to see the homeless even though they had never before visited the United States. They found it to be incomprehensible that a country with such wealth could have so many homeless people living on the streets and in shelters. To be sure, they had similar concerns about the epidemic of crime, youth violence, drugs, social unrest, and racism which ravages so much of our society. But it was the shocking display of homeless individuals that they found most incomprehensible for it contradicted so much of what they had come to understand about freedom in America.

These conversations forced me to realize that a new, more disturbing, perception of America was beginning to take hold around the world. America was no longer being perceived simply as a land of opportunity where hopes and dreams can be realized through personal commitment, hard work, and faith. America was now beginning to appear to the world through electronic images as a nation in decline. And, should that perception come to dominate world public opinion, the vital national security interests of America would be placed in jeopardy in two fundamental respects. On the one hand, if it were concluded that the intrinsic logic of individual freedom leads necessarily to homelessness, social decay, and spiritual alienation—which, it could be argued, the American example indicates—formerly oppressed nations struggling to reshape their future may not judge liberal democracy to be the most attractive political option. On the other hand, if it were concluded that America is in an irreversible process of spiritual decline—which can also be argued—the moral authority and leadership of America in the critical area of human rights would be imperiled and the moral energy that currently unites freedom-loving people around the world could be significantly effaced by an ever-growing stream of violence and conflict. The only way America can dispel these perceptions is to heal alienation at home. Unless this happens, America will by logical necessity become morally and spiritually disengaged from the rest of the world and this growing isolation will signify the death knell of her long-term survival. Without question, the need to heal alienation ranges far beyond America's domestic crisis; it goes to the heart of America's national security.

The Spiritual Causes of Social Dysfunctions

In June 1990, I set out to explore the spiritual dynamics of love and alienation as manifested in the concrete lives of individuals. Much of my time since has been spent on the streets in dialogue with homeless individuals, substance abusers, drug dealers, school dropouts, the jobless, juvenile offenders, prostitutes, felons, unwed mothers, deadbeat fathers, victims of parental violence, runaways, the mentally ill, and others classified as socially dysfunctional.

Surprisingly, the more I came to know these individuals as persons the more it became clear that their story contradicted the basic assumptions commonly held about them. Like the general public and the policy community, I had become so accustomed to seeing and judging them as poor and needy, uneducated and jobless, criminals and prostitutes, substance abusers and deadbeats—or simply as 'lazy' and 'crazy'—that I failed to see the deeper reality that lay behind the 'mask' they presented to the world. Little by little, it became evident that the fundamental cause of their predicament transcended both their social circumstances and material conditions. To be sure, each of them had become socially dysfunctional and economically dependent; that was all too obvious. But, when I perceived this same reality through the stories they told about themselves, a more profound understanding of their social predicament began to emerge.

Indeed, their lives reflected an emptiness at the 'center'—an alienation—which comes from not having been able to satisfy that universal and inherent longing to be at-home-with-others through love in community. For them, alienation runs deep. It is not a mere 'feeling' of depression or hopelessness; nor is it simply a consequence of social and economic dislocations, as commonly presumed. Simply put, spiritual alienation is not an effect. Rather, it is a primary causal force that introduces conflict and chaos into individual behavior. And, when severe enough, it has the potential to cause any of the conditions commonly associated with even the most extreme form of social and material deprivation. As one homeless individual has said: "...even if I were to have a house and job, my situation would not be much different. The problem is that in society I am all alone, isolated from everything and everyone. Until that changes, any effort to get me straight will fail. At least here on the street, I have friends and, right now, that matters more to me than anything else." Why is this so?

The causal origins of social disorders are rooted in the living dynamics of love and alienation which emanate from the existential core of the human person. Within this core, one discovers at a single glance the central impulse of the person—'a crying out for love and community'—and the antithetical, yet primary, condition of the person—an alienation, or separation, from others. It is the struggle of this existential impulse to transcend the primary condition of alienation that forms the dialectical nucleus of all social disorders. To the extent that an individual is alienated from others, he or she will be compelled to do whatever is necessary to create at least some semblance of love or community in his or her life, no matter how imperfect it may be, or how high its cost. Spiritual alienation cannot be tolerated by the human heart.

And yet, the chilling truth is that no individual can escape this aloneness except through the love and mercy of an 'other.' One may cry out to belong, but it is only by being permitted that an individual can transcend alienation. This truth has trememdous implications. For within the heart of every person resides a spiritual inadequacy, an unconditional incompleteness. No individual, regardless of his or her station in life, has an intrinsic capacity to become self-sufficient. The mythology of rampant individualism which shapes and distorts much of our current life is only a mask that enshrouds an inner contradiction and an existential emptiness and aloneness. It is the same mask worn by Citizen Kane whose lust for power denied him the fulfillment he sought. In fact, this unconditional incompleteness can only be alleviated by an act of being permitted and affirmed through the love, compassion, understanding, and mercy of others. Without this act of being permitted, the individual will always remain existentially fragmented and incomplete, and socially dysfunctional behavior will inevitably ensue.

How do the dynamics of dysfunctional behavior begin to unfold? When a young boy, for instance, judges—whether rightly or wrongly—that he is being treated with indifference by family, friends, or neighbors, he will seek 'to belong' elsewhere. If necessary, he will seek 'to belong' on the street, within a gang or a homeless community, or in a drug network. If desperate enough, he may even kill 'to belong.' More than we are willing to admit, then, this restlessness for love defines our innermost being and it is this same restlessness for love that holds the key to understanding and resolving our nation's social crisis.

Three years ago near my hometown in the State of Washington, two fourteen year old boys broke into a neighbor's home one night and stabbed to death an entire family of four. This brutal act was further compounded when they proceeded to beat each victim beyond recognition with a two-by-four. The question is: what drove these boys to commit such acts of brutality? Why? The answer, albeit simple, is hard to comprehend. The simple truth is that these murders were committed as a basic requirement of the rite of passage into a local gang. But, why would these young boys murder their neighbors? Again, the answer is simple, but hard to understand. The truth is that they wanted to belong to this gang. But, why did they want to belong to this gang? Sadly, this gang gave them the only chance they knew to belong with others and to escape the steady pain of being alone and isolated. As one young boy told me: "I have no recollection whatsoever about who I am, or where I have been, and who I am suppose to be or what I was put here for....You know something man, I really don't give a damn where I go right about now. I really don't. And it hurts. It hurts me so much I have cried to the point where I can't even cry anymore." Clearly, spiritual alienation tormented their lives. Eventually, this burden became intolerable. But.....! But.... if they'd just join a gang, they'd gain a family! If they'd just hang out on the street, they'd be with friends. If they'd just 'chill out' with others, or smoke crack, or drink booze, or have sex—or even commit murder—they'd feel less alone and more comfortable than before. Yes, these boys would do anything to be permitted by an 'other' for only in this way could they feel 'at home.'

It is hard to imagine, but street life is compelling. It has a seductiveness as captivating as the songs of the ancient sirens. In a beguiling yet mysterious way, street life helps one who is alienated to alleviate the pain and torment of existential aloneness. It provides them with a sense of community and belonging, a kind of houseless 'home.' It is this sense of 'belonging' or 'being permitted' on the street that helps to explain why homeless individuals often refuse to enter shelters during periods of extreme cold, even against the insistent urging of those who offer help. The truth is they feel more 'comfortable' being on the street—even with its harsh weather and uncertainties—than they would being inside the shelter. To go inside would mean for them not only a loss of personal freedom but also a loss of that street community which they have forged with others. Time and time again, I have been told: "No matter how well off I may become, the street will probably remain the only place where I can feel like I 'belong.' This is where I feel most 'comfortable.' This is where I feel most 'at home.'"

To most observers, statements such as these sound strange. They violate everything we generally assume to be true about human behavior. And yet, strange as they might sound, the emphasis these individuals place on 'belonging' does not go contrary to our deeper understanding of human nature. To 'cry out' for others is the most fundamental of all human inclinations. It defines who we are, what we are for, and why we are here. Indeed, the Christian community believes that God is love and that he has made us for Himself. If this is so—and I am firmly persuaded that it is—it should come as no surprise to learn that socially dysfunctional individuals are also 'crying out' for love and community. As St. Augustine has so eloquently written, their 'hearts are restless' without it. Indeed, more than most of us are willing to admit, a restlessness for love' defines the innermost being of each person and it is this 'restlessness' that is the key to understanding the nature and causes of all social disorders. Simply put, a 'crying out' for love and community is the most profound aspiration of socially dysfunctional individuals and the struggle to realize this yearning is what gives shape to their lives. But, is this not true of us all?

It is a common assumption of our society that socially and economically successful individuals stand outside the range of this existential dynamic. But this is simply not true. Like the socially disaffected, they are also motivated by an existential need to 'belong.' But, unlike the socially disaffected, their quest takes a different form. Rather than joining a community with others—a gang, a drug network, a homeless community—they strive 'to belong' through the attainment of power, wealth, and reputation. In this way, they can gain the respect of others without being committed to others and, for a period of time, their 'restlessness' is mitigated. But, the drive to self-sufficiency—even though it may have carried one to the pinnacle of their profession—can easily cause an individual to be engulfed by an existential condition of 'emptiness.' To be sure, power, wealth, and reputation does generate a mask of happiness. But, behind this facade there often lies a human being without love. Citizen Kane—who had the power, wealth, and reputation to command all but love—clearly symbolizes the 'homeless' individual as they exist in mainstream society. Indeed, his life reveals that a house without love is not a home and those whose house has no love are homeless. Or, to put it another way, a house is made of brick and stone, a home is made of love alone.

Conclusion

What does all this add up to? For one thing, it makes clear that America's predicament is not simply about the socially and economically disadvantaged. Individuals in America today carry greater burdens in their hearts than they do on their backs. Alienation or love, judgment or mercy, pride or humility, aloneness or brotherhood, emptiness or purpose, indifference or compassion—these contradictory qualities depict the unavoidable spiritual decisions each individual must face in every concrete situation throughout their lives. Whether rich or poor, socially placed or displaced, educated or uneducated—whether Caucasian, Afro-American, Hispanic, Asian, or Native American—each person must struggle along an inescapable yet perplexing path in order to come to terms with these transcendent and universal challenges.

The universality of this struggle, and these challenges, serves to remind us that spiritual qualities constitute the very substance of every thought we consider, every action we undertake, and every relationship we establish. Too often we forget how greatly it matters whether our thoughts, actions, and relationships are suffused with indifference or compassion, judgment or mercy, and alienation or love. And yet, it is the dialectical clash of these destructive and perfecting qualities that shape our lives and impact the lives of whomever we encounter. A display of personal indifference, for instance, can not only sour one's own life, but it can easily cause radical and enduring disruption in the lives of others. And, when the dynamics of alienation begin to ripple throughout society, they acquire the potential to unleash a collective impact that can easily fragment and distort the moral fabric of an entire nation, the integrity of its most fundamental institutions—the family, the churches, and the schools—and the 'living dynamics' of its society.

This explains the profound and serious nature of America's social predicament. And yet, for too long we have assumed that this crisis is merely the result of an elemental breakdown of moral values, fundamental institutions, and civil society. To be sure, there is evidence to support such a conclusion. But to explain what has happened is not the same as to explain why it has happened. It is one thing to say, for instance, that America has become the world's leader in most categories of social pathology, but it is quite another matter to ask why this is so. No matter how disruptive, the menacing presence of moral, institutional, and social dysfunctions in America is not self-explanatory. It can only result from a more fundamental human breakdown—a spiritual crisis of the individual and the community.

What desperately needs healing in America, then, is not just this or that individual, or this or that group, or this or that institution, or this or that community, or this or that value. It is the very soul of America—whose life has become suffused with an ethos of alienation—that needs to be healed. But, this 'leprosy of the spirit' cannot be healed through a process of institutional reform, an appeal to traditional values or virtue, or even a rebuilding of civil society. The success of these efforts hinge upon the amelioration of spiritual alienation. Simply put, the only way America will be able to restore integrity to its moral, institutional, and social life is by healing spiritual alienation. And to heal alienation, each of us, and all together, must be willing to extend the gift of self to others through simple acts of love, compassion, understanding, and mercy, and to do so without any conditions or expectations whatsoever.

In conclusion, the transcendent and universal challenge facing America today concerns the quality of relationships each of us has to one another. Americans have always assumed that, once enslaved nations became politically free, a better and more peaceful world would logically follow. In important respects, this optimism has been warranted. The threat of war seems more distant now than at any time since the end of World War I and Americans remain prosperous in a land of boundless opportunity. Nonetheless, a new and unsettling realization is beginning to sweep the land. Individuals are beginning to sense that individual freedom involves more than opportunity, choice, and limited government. It is slowly become apparent that individual freedom also entails living with others in meaningful ways. Indeed, community is the very substance of individual freedom.

But what is community? How does it enrich freedom? The answer is truly simple: community enriches freedom by alleviating the pains of spiritual alienation. Community is not just about having this or doing that in common with others. Community reaches into the very being of the individual and perfects that being through transcendent acts of love, compassion, understanding, and, most importantly, mercy. To be sure, freedom is the central aspiration of the human spirit. But, when it becomes self-centered, freedom becomes cold, indifferent, repelling, and even callous. Without being enriched by the spiritual dynamics of community, freedom is unable to rise above mere opportunity, choice, and personal gain. It can never transcend the hedonistic inclination or the utilitarian claims imposed on others, thereby leaving those who are bound to this context little else but to journey into spiritual emptiness and some form of human tragedy. The bottom line is that freedom and community are inseparable. Only to the extent that the spiritual forces of community become the substance of family, institutions, and society—and the international order—will individuals be able to realize their yearning to be free because at last they will existentially belong.

The Modern Western Family: Trends and Implications from the United States

Patrick Fagan
The Heritage Foundation
Washington, D.C.

John Paul II has called all Christians to set about building a culture of love. He gives us the remedy, and the means. In this paper I propose to give a partial diagnosis in sociological terms of the underlying disease: the increasing alienation of man from woman, deep within the building block of society, deep within the family. This alienation is analogous to HIV in the human body... it is altering the basic cell. *Familiaris Consortio* and *Veritatis Splendor* give a much deeper diagnosis. However a sociological and demographic picture also helps. The social sciences can inform the discourse on natural law. Such, indeed, is their purpose and function.

Western democracies all suffer in various degrees from problems stemming from the breakdown in the family, which is really a breakdown in marriage. While the instrumental institutions of the economy and government function robustly by historical standards, the relational institutions of family, church and school are all showing serious weaknesses. A look at United States' data, which is a relatively rich body of information, gives many lessons that can be learned by its own citizens and many others.

Americans are increasingly anxious about the breakdown of the basic institutions of society. Many once-friendly and peaceful neighborhoods are now threatening and dangerous. Particularly alarming is the breakdown of marriage and the family. Marriage and the stable two-parent family form the centerbeam of society, but soaring rates of divorce and out-of-wedlock births are destroying this crucial institution and weakening the development of the next generation. This means more welfare dependence, more crime, more health and behavioral problems, lower educational achievement, and the prospect of daunting obstacles in later life.

I. Family Breakdown

First we will look at the weaknesses, for it is easier for most people to see strengths after they have contemplated weaknesses. The cost of the good sometimes causes some people to dismiss it. However the cost of the bad are even higher and that may have some salutary effect on the debate.

The weakening of the family takes two demographic forms: out-of-wedlock births and divorce.

A clear picture of the proportion of children being affected by broken family life emerges by adding the number of children entering broken families, either through out-of-wedlock birth or through divorce every year, and plotting them as a proportion of the total number of children born into the United States that year. This ratio has grown from 12 per 100 in 1950 to over 58 per 100 in 1992. Sadly, we must conclude that American parents have massively diminished the strength of their families for the last 2 generations of children. The effects are becoming more clearly documented with time. As a proportion of all out-of-wedlock births have been rising steadily, from under 4 percent in 1950 to 31 percent in 1993. America has one of the highest total out-of-wedlock birth rates and *the* highest teenage out-of-wedlock birth rate in the world. Divorce reached its highest rate in 1978, dropped only slightly thereafter and has held steady since then. Americans divorce at the highest rate among all nations in the world.

Rejection Ratio: Number of Children Entering a Broken Family Each Year for Every 100 Children Born that year

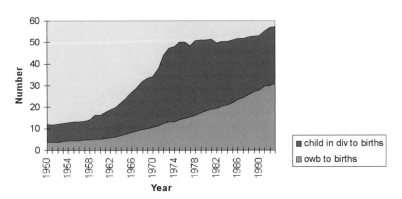

i) Out-of-Wedlock Births

The continuing rise in the illegitimacy rate is propelled by three factors:

- A decline in the portion of women of childbearing age who are married;
- An increase in the birth or fertility rate among non-married women; and
- A decline in the birth or fertility rate among married women.

Historically, illegitimate births hovered at low rates. In recent decades, however, this pattern has changed radically. According to the most recent statistics released by the Center for Health Statistics at the U.S. Department of Health and Human Services, illegitimacy continues to rise rapidly and marriage continues to decline across the United States.

73

Recently released US government data show that out-of-wedlock births have actually decreased minimally in the last two years. This may be a blip or the beginning of an arresting of the rate of out-of-wedlock childbearing.

1992 ...30.1%
1993 ...31.0%
1994 ...32.6%
1995 ...32.4%
1996 ...32.2%

Trends in OWB and Within Marriage Births

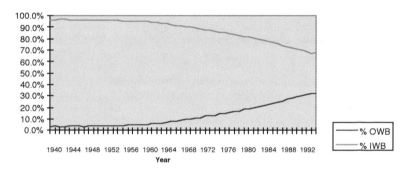

Among whites in 1993, 23.6 percent of births were out-of-wedlock, up from 11 percent in 1980. Among blacks, 68.7 percent of births were out-of-wedlock in 1993, up from 58 percent in 1980.

For blacks especially, in certain parts of the country the rates are alarmingly high: as high as 82 % for blacks in Wisconsin in the early 1990's, and in the high seventy percent range for blacks in most of the states around the Great Lakes. For all groups in all parts of the country, the trend is the same: steadily upwards at similar rates of increase.

ii) Divorce

Divorce also is a major contributor to single parent families. The number of children effected now seems to have steadied off at a little over 1 million children per year.

Divorce reached its highest rate in 1978 and has dropped only slightly since then. Americans divorce at the highest rate among all nations in the world.[1]

Since 1972, over a million children per year have suffered the pains and effects of the breakup of their parents' marriages.

Number of Children Under 18 Years of Age, Affected by Divorce, 1950 - 1993

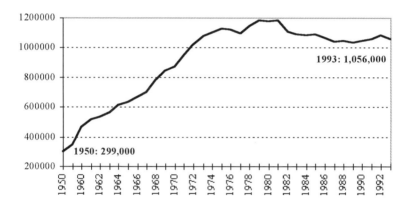

iii) Effects of Broken Family Life on Children :

Children pay a high price for their parents' weaknesses. The overall effects of out-of-wedlock births and divorce are all negative with both conditions tending to push children in the same directions (with slightly different rates for some outcomes).

- lowered health for newborns and increases their chances of dying;

75

- retarded cognitive, especially their verbal, development;
- lowered educational achievement;
- lowered job attainment;
- increased behavior problems;
- lowered impulse control;
- warped social development;
- Increased welfare dependency; Some 92 percent of children on welfare today are from broken families.[2]
- increased child and spouse abuse;
- increased crime in the local community;
- increased chances of being physically or sexually abused.

As the following chart shows, the children of the poor are those most affected by the breakdown in marriage.

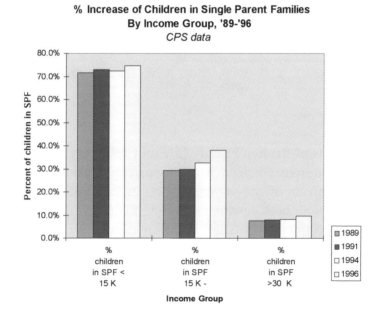

% Increase of Children in Single Parent Families By Income Group, '89-'96
CPS data

iv) The Effects of Divorce on Adults[3]

A broken family has damaging impacts on adults, too. Life expectancy, physical health, psychological health, and the economic well-being of the adults involved are all reduced. In the case of divorced adults, they exhibit:

Shorter life expectancy.

Married people have consistently lower death rates from disease, suicide, and accident mortality.[4] The death rate among nonsmoking divorced men is almost the same as it is for men who smoke at least one pack of cigarettes a day. Overall, the premature death rate is four times higher among divorced white men than among their married counterparts.[5]

Poorer physical health.

Divorced and separated people experience acute conditions such as infectious and parasitic diseases, respiratory illnesses, digestive system illnesses, and severe injuries in greater numbers than other marital status groups.[6]

Poorer psychological health.

The divorced have higher levels of stress and psychiatric disorders (depression, for example), which in turn also have a profound impact on their physical well-being, including depressed immunological capacities.[7]

Lower economic well-being.

Women who experience an increase in income after divorce are either those who are very poor, and who go on AFDC, or those who work much longer hours after divorce than they did before divorce.[8]

While married black Americans have been moving steadily out of poverty (the poverty rate among this group, in 1994 figures, is now 11.4 percent) and are closing in on the white married poverty rate (8.3 percent), the rate is still 53.9 percent for black American female-headed families five times the rate for married black Americans.[9]

II. Community Breakdown

When the rate of single parent families in a community reaches about 30 percent the community begins to break down, and changes from being a support to being a danger to the development of children. and the rate of crime in the community begins to soar.

The collapse, almost extinction, of two-parent families in poor inner-city neighborhoods has contributed heavily to the collapse of those neighborhoods. The absence of fathers means there is no adult male financial support, guiding hand, or protection for children. The result: gangs of young men driven by a destructive credo, young girls vulnerable to abuse, children having children, and mindless, violent crime.

In addition, institutions in poor neighborhoods that once provided help and guidance to those lacking it at home have been crowded out by the burgeoning welfare state. Caring and knowing local people have been replaced by armies of professional social workers and bureaucrats who emphasize rights and rules, not freedom and responsibility. Effective faith-based solutions to educational and social deficiencies are barred from receiving government funds to carry out their work and if they are able to receive support, it is often only by giving up their religious message. [10]

State-by-state analysis indicates that, in general, a 10 percent increase in the percentage of children living in single-parent homes (including divorces) accompanies a 17 percent increase in juvenile crime.[11]

High-crime neighborhoods tend to be single-parent neighborhoods. Researchers long ago observed that violent crime, among both teenagers and adults, is concentrated most heavily in urban neighborhoods characterized by a very high proportion of single-parent families.[12] Today's researchers, like those before them, find that a neighborhood composed mainly of single-parent families invariably is a chaotic, crime-ridden community,[13] where gangs assume control.[14] In these chaotic conditions, parental supervision of adolescent and pre-adolescent children is almost impossible.[15] In turn, children living in these neighborhoods are more likely to learn, accept, and use physical violence to satisfy their wants and needs.[16]

For example:

- The last 15 years have seen an extraordinary increase in community violence in most major American cities which, despite recent moderately good news, has not been rolled back nearly enough. In 1990, the homicide rates increased in Boston by over 40 percent over the previous year; in Denver, by 29 percent; in Chicago, Dallas, and New Orleans, by more than 20 percent; in Los Angeles, by 16 percent; and in New York, by 11 percent.[17]

- In 1988, nationwide firearm death rates for all teenagers for the first time exceeded the total for all other natural causes of death combined, and black male teens were 11 times more likely than their white counterparts to be killed by guns.[18] Thus, despite the good news of a recent drop in crime, the decrease has to continue for a long time for the nation to return to past levels of safety and peace.

- Crime has risen sharply within inner-city schools, making places of education "no-go" areas for many children. "Twenty percent of high school students now carry a firearm, knife, razor, club, or some other weapon on a regular basis."[19]

- According to the National League of Cities, school violence during the past year resulted in student death and injury in 41 percent of American cities with a population of 100,000 or more.[20]

- "In 1991, 134,000 teenagers used cocaine once a week or more and 580,000 teenagers used marijuana once a week or more. In addition, 454,000 junior and senior high school students were weekly binge drinkers."[21]

- Approximately 900 teachers throughout the nation are threatened with bodily harm, and nearly 40 are physically attacked, each hour of the school day. Some 160,000 students miss school daily because of intimidation or fear of bodily harm.[22]

- A 1993 USA Weekend survey on school disruption revealed that nearly 40 percent of students nationwide think schools are unsafe.[23]

In recent years, 1995 and 1996, these crime trends have been reversed ... by building more prisons and through more effective police work, incarcerating increasing numbers of habitual criminals.[24]

If one looks for the single biggest contributor to the rise in crime, two factors stand out in the research literature: the breakdown of the family and the rise in illegitimacy.

III. Some Underlying Cultural Dynamics

i) Changes in the Sexual Mores:

The most fundamental change in society began to occur in the first third of this century: severing of the child as the ultimate end of the sexual act. As a result our society has increasingly become a hostile place for children, and we must now confront the fact that for the young the United States is predominantly a culture of rejection.

In 1930, at the Anglican Church Lambeth Conference, a Christian denomination officially sanctioned contraception for the first time in the history of modern Christendom. Despite the immediate outcry by most other Christians, and even by the secular press, the acceptance of contraception as a morally permitted act quickly spread through nearly all denominations. By the late 1940's the idea had turned into act and American married couples were contracepting in growing numbers. By the 1960's the children of these contracepting couples led the sexual revolution, logically rejecting the need for marriage as the context for the sexual act, when the purposes of the sexual act no longer included conception and the child. By the 1970's the next generation, needing a backstop for unwanted pregnancies, enshrined the "woman's right to choose"... abortion...ensuring the ability to pursue sex for pleasure without the natural constraints of the ensuing obligations which the child brings. A generation later in the 1990's we have the rise of homosexual rights, a logical extension of the view of the sexual act as a means for pleasure ... where one person's pleasure may not be another's.

From being rare early in the century, contraception has become widespread and habitual.

If we assume[25] that there is but one partner sterilized in each marriage then the following picture emerges:

% of Married Women Contracepting
Source: Pratt WF, Peterson, LS, Piccinino LJ,:Trends in Contraceptive Practice and Contraceptive Choice: Unioted States 1965-1990: Unpublished . Received from Stephanie Ventura NCHS May 1997

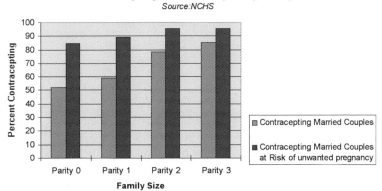

1990 Contracepting Married Couples by Family Size
Source:NCHS

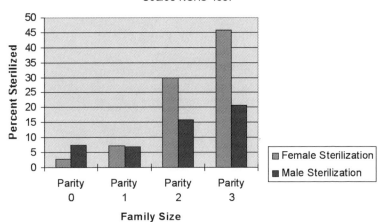

Sterilization in Marriage by Family Size
Source NCHS 1997

Total of Huband + Wife Sterilizations

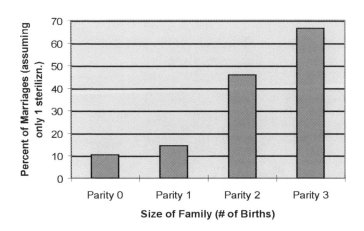

The practice of contraception unanchors man. The sexual act, as long as it is open to life, has the effect of keeping man, at minimum, oriented towards "the other". Without that minimum man becomes self-centered in that most pleasurable of all activities.

This inner psychological rearrangement of attitudes and heart spills quickly into a changed relationship with the spouse, the opposite sex and with children, resulting in divorce, out-of-wedlock births, abortions, and abandoned children.

Radical changes for society result: from being ordered unto children and building the future to being centered on the individual self, and on present gratifications.

ii) Abortion

In terms of family breakdown and the threat to children of not growing up in a family once conceived, the different rates of abortion within and outside of marriage contribute to the severing of society's former linking of children, marriage, and sexual

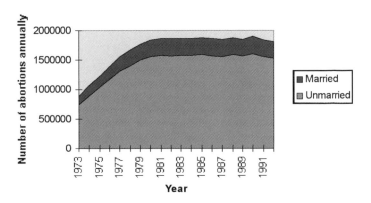

Estimate of Abortions Within and Outside of Marriage

intercourse. There is only one large sample survey, reported in 1989 by the Alan Guttmacher Institute, which gives a snapshot of the rates of abortion within and outside of marriage.[26]

Abortion Rates 1988:
Married, living with husband present 18.5 percent
Separated 6.4 percent
Divorced 11.2 percent
Never married 63.3 percent

If this ratio is applied (as the best approximation we have from research) to the incidence of abortion since 1973, then the following picture emerges: The vast proportion of abortions occur among those committed neither to the child nor to a spouse; in other words, among the unattached. The best way to reduce abortion is to reduce sexual intercourse outside of marriage. This means a cultural change that depends primarily on the effectiveness of the family, the church, and schools at their tasks; such a change is not possible through government action alone.

iii) Family Time Famine

Getting adequate after-tax family income has become relatively more difficult for married parents with children. Consequently family time has suffered as work outside the home becomes more common for mothers of school-going children.

- By 1990 on average, parents are available 10 hours less per week to their children than they were in 1980, and a full 40 percent less than they were in 1965. [27]

- A Massachusetts Mutual 1993 poll found that 33 percent of parents say they don't spend enough time with preschool children, and 46 percent say do not spend enough time with teenagers.[28]

- A 1990 *Los Angeles Times* poll found that 57 percent of all fathers and 55 percent of all mothers felt guilty about spending too little time with their children. The poll also found that 73 percent of all married couples would have one parent stay home full time with the children "if money were not an issue".[29]

- Adequate time with his parents is critical for the development of every child, especially their self-esteem and confidence. As Harvard University child psychiatrist, Robert Coles, puts it: "The frenzied need of children to have possessions isn't only a function of the ads they see on TV. It's a function of their hunger for what they aren't getting—their parents' time."[30]

- Reflecting the growing concern about the time

famine, a Yankelovich poll found a big jump (from 39 percent to 57 percent) between 1989 and 1990 in mothers who would give up work indefinitely if no longer needed the money.[31]

- Reflecting the concern about mother absence a 1993 poll by Family Research Council: 89 percent of parents believe that their children would do better if cared for by their mother rather than by day-care providers. Similarly an increasing number of parents think too many children are being raised in child care.[32]

Commenting on one of the by-products in this attenuation of attention to children Dr. James Allen Fox, Dean of the College of Criminal Justice at Northeastern University in Boston, stated at a recent Congressional hearing:

I think it's a matter of supervision...one of the important elements that we are not talking about.... For example at this point 57% of the children in this country do not have full time parental supervision.... Almost 45% of the juvenile violent crimes occur between 3:00 in the afternoon and dinnertime. [They] are unsupervised in the neighborhood."[33]

Over the next ten years we will have a 23% increase in the number of teenagers in this country.... We'll have a 29% increase in the number of black teenagers, a 50% percent increase in the number of Latino teenagers. I'm really concerned. I think this is the calm before the storm.[34]

iv) Changes in Mother's Availability to Children:

There is an obvious depletion in the time available to U.S. children from their mothers. The effect of more than twenty hours of absence per week is to increase the risk of attenuation of early infant attachment which in turn further increases the risk of the child's ability to form close and satisfying intimate relationships in the teen years and in adulthood.[35]

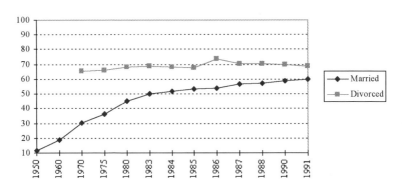

Working Mothers Absent From Their Children _Under Age Six_
1950 - 1991

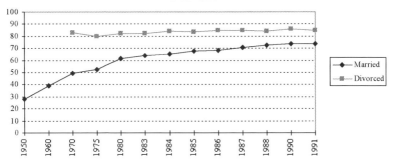

Working Mothers Absent From Their Children
Ages 6 - 17
1950 - 1991

IV. Government's Role In The Breakdown

i) Tax Take on the Family

Families also have come under assault from the tax system. Today the federal income tax takes one-fourth of the income of the average married family with children and state and local taxes increase the total government take to 38 percent.[36] This compares with just two percent in federal taxes paid by a similar family just after World War II. The rise in taxation is due in large part to the erosion, through inflation, of the personal exemption and the sharp rise in payroll taxes.

The next generation is already under assault from the present government's spending habits. The national debt is a $70,000 mortgage on the back of every child under 18. Instead of allowing Americans to pass a patrimony of wealth on to their children, entitlement programs are eating their future earnings. Children have become not dependents, but providers.

ii) The Poor And Recent Forms Of Welfare

To a significant extent, government programs and policies have contributed to this collapse. The incentives within welfare programs over the last 30 years have discouraged two-parent families among the poor. These programs also have discouraged work and responsible behavior.

The US welfare problem is not on the material level, where rather than failing we have succeeded at a phenomenal level in providing for our poor. Nicholas Eberstat of Harvard University recently put it succinctly : "We have created in our midst a class of prosperous paupers." [37]

V. Serious Disorders Against the Common Good

The utilitarian materialist culture has spawned a culture of rejection, the rejection of men and women of each other, illustrated in out-of-wedlock births and divorce, but resulting in massively increased burdens of rejection and alienation on children. This rejection leads, logically, to a number of patterns that are serious threats to the common good: child abuse, crime, drug addiction, sexually transmitted diseases.

i) Child Abuse and family structure:

From British data,[38] with *some* confirmation in American studies (where the issue is largely unexamined), we can say that, compared to the traditional, intact, married family, the rates of abuse of children may be as much as six times higher in blended (divorced and remarried) families, thirteen times higher in single mother-living-alone families, twenty times higher in families where both natural parents live together in cohabitation, and thirty-three times higher when the mother cohabits with a boyfriend.

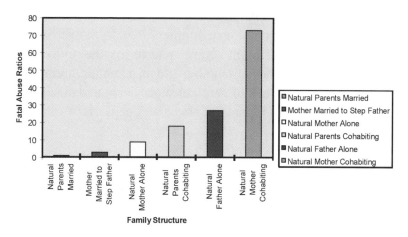

Family Structure and Fatal Abuse Risk Ratios

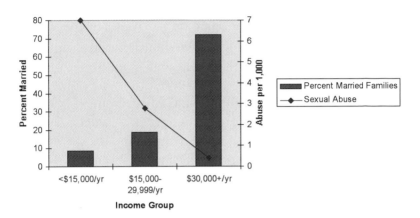

Sex Abuse Rate and % Married

ii) **Crime:**

The five stages in the development of most serious criminals most frequently have their beginnings in the abandonment of the child by the father. Add abuse and neglect in early childhood, and the child is on his way to a serious life of crime.

Stage One, early childhood years:

Parental neglect and abandonment in early home life are characterized by different combinations of the following: fatherlessness, absence of a mother's love, parental fighting and domestic violence, lack of parental supervision and discipline, rejection of the child, parental abuse and neglect, or criminal parents.

Stage Two, mid childhood years:

The embryonic gang emerges as young, unsocialized, aggressive children, rejected by their more normal peers, seek and find other alienated children, fail at school, lose interest in education, and begin to run wild.

Stage Three, early teenage years:

The embryonic gang of grade school changes into a gang of tough, exploitative teenagers who gradually become more and more expert in crime.

Stage Four, mid teenage years:

Violence emerges as a way of life within the gang as the more expert learn to do their crime without getting caught.

Stage Five: late teenage years, early adulthood:

A new baby is born to the now-criminal young father, who stays with the child's mother for a while before abandoning her and her child. The mother comes from a background similar to the young criminal father's.

The more single-parent families we put in place, the more likely it is that increasing numbers of children will experience this pathway to crime. Overall, a 10 percent increase in illegitimacy leads to a 17 percent increase in serious violent crime (see chart below). With the continued rise in illegitimacy, we will see more and more violent criminals coming onto our streets as they reach their mid-teenage years. And with the appearance of these criminals, we will lose more and more of our everyday freedoms, and will be forced to pay other huge social

RISE IN CRIME RATE AND CHILDREN IN SINGLE-PARENT FAMILIES: 1960-1991

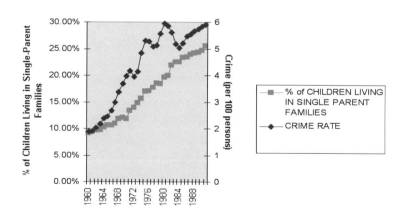

and economic costs.

iii) Drug Use (on the Rise Again)

The number of Americans using illicit drugs plunged from a peak of 24.7 million in 1979 to 11.4 million in 1992. The so-called casual use of cocaine fell by 79 percent between 1985 and 1992, while monthly cocaine use fell 55 percent between 1988 and 1992 alone, from 2.9 million to 1.3 million users.

This is deadly serious business, since 12-17 year olds who use marijuana are 85 more times more likely to graduate to cocaine than those who abstain from marijuana.[39]

Jim Burke, chairman of Partnership for a Drug-Free America, stated that roughly one in thirteen of those who take drugs become addicts:

> "In 1962 less than 4 million Americans had ever tried an illegal drug in their lifetime. In 1992, one generation later, 80 million had tried illegal drugs.... Of the 80 million we now have 6 million addicts.... If you go back to 1962 we only had 300,000 addicts. The numbers are very clear: twenty times more triers, twenty times more addicts.... We know what works. Children are just as rational as adults. If they believe that the risk goes up in using drugs, their usage goes down. Social disapproval and perception of risk are the two drivers."[40]

The drug situation is getting worse on all three major indicators among teenagers:

- Perception of harm or risk has decreased;
- Disapproval of drugs among teenage peers has decreased; and
- Availability of drugs has increased.

Burke also stated: "If you go back to the epidemic before [1978] when we normalized drugs, the average age of trial [first use] in that period was around 16. The average age of trial today is 13.... and current marijuana is three to five times stronger."[41]

V. Strengths of Society

i) Marriage

Marriage, and all that goes to make it possible, has extraordinary explanatory power when one looks at rates of crime, welfare, joblessness, educational failure, drug addiction, and health problems. For instance the differences in crime rates among blacks and whites disappear when marriage is factored in. Among married families, black or white, the crime rate is similar and low. Among broken families, black or white, the crime rate is similar and high.

ii) Adoption

The benefits of growing up in a two parent family are again illustrated in the case of adopted children. Adopted children do as well or better than their non-adopted counterparts. [42] Adopted children *score higher* than their middle class two parent counterparts on indicators of school performance, social competency, optimism, and volunteerism.[43] Adopted adolescents are generally less depressed than children of single parents and are less involved in alcohol abuse, vandalism, group fighting, police trouble, weapon use, and theft;[44] they score higher on self-esteem, confidence in their own judgment, self-directedness, positive view of others, and feelings of security within their families. [45, 46] On health measures, adopted children and of intact families share similarly high scores, and both those groups score significantly higher on these measures than children raised by single parents.[47] Adopted children do well at school. In 1988, only 7 percent of children adopted in infancy repeated a grade.[48] By contrast 33 percent of children whose mothers had never married repeated a grade. Adoptive parents are also less likely to divorce.[49]

iii) The Strength Of The Family Intertwined With The Practice Of Religion.

From medical and social science research literature we can state clearly that the strength of the family unit is intertwined with the practice of religion.

- Church goers are more likely to be married, less likely to be divorced or single, and are more likely to manifest high levels of satisfaction in marriage.
- Church attendance is the most important predictor of marital stability and happiness.
- The regular practice of religion is instrumental in helping poor persons move out of poverty. Regular church attendance helps young people in particular to escape the poverty of inner-city life.
- Religious beliefs and practices contribute substantially to the formation of personal moral criteria, and sound moral judgment.
- Regular religious practice generally inoculates individuals against a host of social problems including suicide, drug abuse, out-of-wedlock births, crime, and divorce.
- Regular practice of religion has powerful mental health impacts including less depression (a modern epidemic), more self-esteem, and greater family and marital happiness.
- In repairing damage caused by alcoholism, drug addictions, and marital breakdown, religious beliefs and practices are a major source of strength and recovery.
- Regular practice of religion is good for personal physical health: longevity, recovery from illness, and lessened incidence of many killer diseases.

"Middletown", one of the classic sociological research projects of the century, studied the lives of inhabitants of a typical American town, first in the 1920s and for the third time in the 1980s. Howard Bahr and Bruce Chadwick, professors of sociology at Brigham Young University concluded in 1985 from the latest round of follow-up research that "There is a relationship between family solidarity—family health if you will—and church affiliation and activity. Middletown [church-going] members were more likely to be married, remain married and to be highly satisfied with their marriages and to have more children. ...The great divide between marriage status, marriage satisfaction and family size is ... between those who identify with a church or denomination and those who do not." [50] The strong intergenerational transmission of religious affiliation and practice found in the Middletown studies has been repli-cated by Professor Arland Thornton of the Institute for Social Research at the University of Michigan. He concluded in 1989 that "These data indicate a strong intergenerational transmis-sion of religious involvement. Attendance at religious services is also very stable within generations across time." [51]

Summing up the findings Professor Allan Bergin, a re-search psychologist who was honored by the American Psycho-logical Association with its top award in 1990 said in his acceptance speech: "Some religious influences have a modest impact whereas another portion seem like the mental equivalent of nuclear energy." For a national sample of young adults which the Department of Labor has been tracking for twenty years the combined effects of marriage and worship on their income levels (just one issue among many) can be seen in figure 2 below. There is a 50 percent difference between the lowest and highest group, between those who grew up in a broken, non-worshipping family, and those who grew up in an intact, regularly worshipping family.

Family/Church Background in 1979 & 1982;
Income in 1993
Source: NLSY 1993

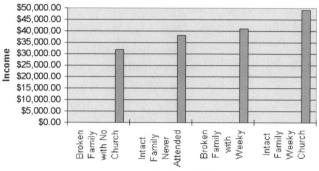

Family/ Church Attendance

From the social sciences literature we can say that the child does best nested in the family, the family does best nested in marriage, and marriage does best nested in religious worship of God. Where all four patterns are present we will have many more happy children, families and communities, and less crowded courts. The professional literature indicates what common sense and life experience also teach: two of the most powerful ways out of our social problems are life-long marriage and the regular worship of God.

VII. Summary

Personal rejection by those very close to us is one of the most painful forms of suffering. In adults it frequently causes depression, irritability, loss of interest and productivity in work, and lack of concentration. It is related to a host of psychiatric illnesses.

Birth outside of marriage, as well as divorce, is structural rejection...by the parents of each other, and (most frequently) of the child by the father. For children the effects of weakened family life take multiple serious forms, and the evidence is incontrovertibly negative.

The attenuation of time spent in conversation, which is time spent in knowing and enjoying the other, is weakening the weave and woof of the human community. Many factors go into this, from transportation technologies, television, travel and relocation, and the pursuit of increased income. Children suffer the effects of this attenuation most, for conversation is the lifeblood of the developing child, the source not only of knowledge, of relationships but also of a truer and firmer sense of the self, without which the future adult cannot give as much to others. And thus the cycle of alienation deepens.

Increasingly the economy, adapting to the desires of citizens, is itself becoming an end rather than a means, and family life is increasingly adapting to the needs of the economy rather than the economy adapting to the needs of the family.

Other non-benign factors contribute: contraception, which ultimately causes an inversion of the self unto the self; abortion, and divorce are now structures of sin that are publicly protected.

All of these patterns add up to the United States being a very dangerous place for children today:

The U.S. Rejection Ratio :

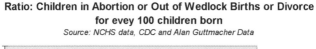

Ratio: Children in Abortion or Out of Wedlock Births or Divorce for evey 100 children born
Source: NCHS data, CDC and Alan Guttmacher Data

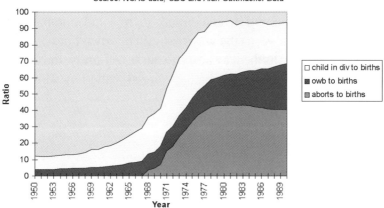

The good news however is that the suffering resulting from this alienation and rejection is having its sobering effect. More and more people question the present direction of US society and more and more are discussing the alternatives. The recent change in the out-of-wedlock birth rate may be the beginning of a trend. Abortions are also decreasing. Divorce is increasingly being questioned. Out-of-wedlock births are no longer seen as just another alternative, but as deleterious for the child.

Americans are a pragmatic people and generally need to have a project underway. The next project may well be the restoration of marriage and family life. That in turn may alter the utilitarian culture for the better. It is the beginning of a race between decay and rebirth. Only the future will tell how the society of the United States will fare, but there are many lessons for other nations who want to keep their own societies strong.

The central lessons to be learned from all the social research that is coming from the United States is that children, the future society of any nation, thrive in close family life; that family life thrives in the married family and that married families thrive on the regular community worship of the Creator. These are the ingredients of a humane and strong society.

All this data fits with the analysis of John Paul II, who takes over from here and leads on to the remedies that are simple and profound: the mysteries of Creation, the Divine order in the family and in the relationship between man and woman, the mystery of Redemption and grace, mercy and compassion, repentance and love, as the ways to build our own families well here on earth and as the way home to our final family, the family of the Blessed Trinity, to which we are all called by adoption.

Notes

1. "Children's Well Being: An International Comparison," Bureau of the Census, 1990, pp. 8, 9, 35.

2. Department of Health and Human Services, Administration for Families, *AFDC FlashReports*, September 1995

3. Summarized from recent overview of the divorce literature as published in David B. Larson, James P. Swyers, and Susan S. Larson, *The Costly Consequences of Divorce: Assessing the Clinical, Economic and Public Health Impacts of Marital Disruption in the United States* (Rockville, Md.: National Institute for Healthcare Research, 1995).

4. *Ibid.*, pp. 43-49.

5. *Ibid.*, pp. 58-59.

6. *Ibid.*, pp. 58-61.

7. *Ibid.*, pp. 62-70.

8. *Ibid.*, pp. 7275.

9. Bureau of the Census, "Income, Poverty, and Valuation of Noncash Benefits: 1994," P60189, Table B7.

10. Joeseph Loconte: "The Seduction of the Samaritan" Pioneer Institute, Boston, 1997

11. Patrick F. Fagan, "The Real Root Causes of Violent Crime: The Breakdown of Marriage, Family and Community," *Heritage Foundation Backgrounder* No. 1026, March 17, 1995. pp. 910.

12. Shaw and McKay, *Juvenile Delinquency and Urban Areas* (Chicago: University of Chicago, 1942), cited in

Jeffrey Fagan and Sandra Wexler, "Family Origins of Violent Delinquents," *Criminology*, Vol. 25, No. 3 (1987), pp. 643-669.

13. Douglas Smith and G. Roger Jarjoura, "Social Structure and Criminal Victimization," *Journal of Research in Crime and Delinquency*, Vol. 25 (February 1988), pp. 2752; M. Anne Hill and June O'Neill, *Underclass Behavior in the United States: Measurement and Analysis of Determinants* (New York: City University of New York, Baruch College, March 1990).

14. Fagan and Wexler, "Family Origins of Violent Delinquents."

15. A.J. Reis, Jr., "Why Are Communities Important in Understanding Crime?" in *Communities and Crime* (Chicago: University of Chicago, 1986), pp. 133.

16. Elton J. Jackson, Charles Tittle, and M.J. Burke, "Offensespecific Models of Differential Association," paper presented at annual meeting of the American Society of Criminology, 1984, cited in Fagan and Wexler, "Family Origins of Violent Delinquents;" Rodney Stark, "Deviant Places: A Theory of the Ecology of Crime," *Criminology*, Vol. 25 (1987), pp. 893-909.

17. G. Escobar, "Washington Area's 703 Homicides in 1990 Set a Record," *The Washington Post*, January 2, 1991, p. A1.

18. K.K. Christofel, "Violent Death and Injury in U.S. Children and Adolescents," *American Journal of Disease Control*, Vol. 144 (1990), pp. 697-706; John E. Richters and Pedro E. Martinez, "The NIMH Community Violence Project: Children as Victims of and Witnesses to Violence," *Psychiatry*, Vol. 56 (1993), pp. 735.

19. William Bennett, *The Index of Leading Cultural Indicators: Facts and Figures on the State of American Society* (New York: Simon and Schuster, 1994), p. 31.

20. Associated Press, "School Survey Finds Violence All Over; Big Cities Are Worst," *The Washington Post*, November 2, 1994, p. A17.

21. Bennett, *The Index of Leading Cultural Indicators*, p. 42.

22. Associated Press, "100,000 Students Carry Guns, Teacher Group Says," *The Baltimore Sun*, January 15, 1993.

23. Leslie Ansley, "Safety in Schools: It Just Keeps Getting Worse," USA Weekend, August 1315, 1993, pp. 46.

24. William J. Bratton: "Cutting Crime And Restoring Order: What America Can Learn From New York's Finest"; Heritage Lecture #573, October 15, 1996. The Heritage Foundation, Washington D.C.

25. an assumption open to question and one likely not completely true: the aggregated figure assumes that there is only one sterilization per couple.

26. Stanley K. Henshaw et al., "Characteristics and Private Contraceptive Use of U.S. Abortion Patients," *Family Planning Perspectives*, Vol. 20, No. 4 (July/August 1989), p. 162.

27. from research on personal time diaries by sociologist John Robinson of U MD. In William R. Mattox Jr. "The Parent Trap" *Policy Review*,#55, Winter 1991, pp. 6-13.

28. Family Research Council: "Family Time: What Americans Want."

29. *ibid.*

30. Quoted by William R. Mattox Jr. "The Parent Trap" *Policy Review*,#55, Winter 1991, p. 10.

31. *ibid*

32. Times Mirror poll 1990, quoted in "Family Time: What Americans Want." Family Research Council, Washington DC.

33. Dr. James Allen Fox, testimony at hearing on juvenile drug use, Committee on the Judiciary, U.S. Senate, December 20, 1995.

34. *Ibid.*

35. Virginia Colin, "Infant Attachment: What we know, A Literature Review" HHS/ ASPE Washington DC April 1991, page 81. "Babies who start day care early in life and spend more than 20 hours per week in non-parental care develop avoidant attachments somewhat more often than other babies do."

36. Robert Rector, "Reducing the Crushing Tax Burden on America's Families," *Heritage Foundation Backgrounder* No. 981, March 7, 1994.

37. Nicholas Eberstat: "The Tyranny of Numbers: Mismeasurement and Misrule" AEI Press, Washington DC 1995

38. Robert Whelan: "Broken Homes and Battered Children: A study of the relationship between child abuse and family type." Family Education Trust, Oxford, 1994

39. Senator Orrin Hatch, testimony at hearing on juvenile drug use, Comittee on the Judiciary, U.S. Senate, December 20, 1995

40. Jim Burke, testimony at hearing on juvenile drug use, Committee on the Judiciary, U.S. Senate, December 20, 1995.

41. *Ibid.*

42. Peter L.Benson, Anu R. Shorma, and Eugene C. Roehlkepartain, "Growing Up Adopted — A portrait of adolescents and their families," Search Institute, Minneapolis, MN, June 1994.

43. Peter Benson, *op. cit.*

44. Benson, P. op cit.

45. Marquis, Kathleen S. and Richard A. Detweiler, "Does Adoption Mean Different? An Attributional Analysis," *Journal of Personality and Social Psychology,* Vol. 48, No. 4, 1985, pp. 1054-1066.

46. An interesting anomaly has emerged from an analysis of adoption studies. While clinical studies have traditionally shown adopted adolescents to be over-represented in psychiatric settings, the same occurred here but these adolescents were found not to have emotional or psychological problems. Adopted adults are less likely to receive treatment than the general population. This seeming contradiction occurs because adoptive parents are more likely to refer their adopted children for possible treatment. Of all adopted children referred by parents for clinical treatment only 27 percent had a clinical diagnosis. The remainder, almost three quarters, received counseling for normal adolescent issues. Leslie Stein and Janet Hoopes, Washington, DC: Child Welfare League of America, 1985.

47. Nicholas Zill, Ph.D., "Behavior and Learning Problems Among Adopted Children: Findings from a U.S.

National Survey of Child Health," Washington, DC: Child Trends, Inc., paper presented at the Society for Research in Child Development, April 27, 1985.

48. *Ibid.*

49. *Unmarried Parents Today*, Washington, DC, National Committee For Adoption, June 25, 1985.

50. Howard M. Bahr, Bruce A. Chadwick : "Religion and Family in Middletown, USA" *Journal of Marriage and Family*, May 1985 PP 407- 414

51. Thornton, Arland and Donald Camburn, "Religious Participation and Adolescent Sexual Behavior and Attitudes," *Journal of Marriage and the Family* 51 (August 1989): 641-653.

PART IV

BUILDING THE CULTURE OF LIFE THROUGH THE FAMILY

Building the Culture of Life Through the Family

John M. Haas
The National Catholic Bioethics Center
(Formerly the Pope John Center)
Boston, Massachusetts

The broad range of issues which largely define what our Holy Father has called the "culture of death" seem in a singular way to be arrayed against the family. The list is long and all too familiar: contraception, abortion, partial-birth abortion, infanticide, homosexual activity, out-of-wedlock births, the HIV/AIDS epidemic, the historically high incidence of sexually transmitted disease, divorce, child abuse, spousal abuse, even physician-assisted suicide and euthanasia, insofar as these have arisen because support systems and nurturing care are no longer provided by the family. All these phenomena are fundamentally death-dealing. And no other social institution than the family seems to be so intensely the focus of their destructive force. Since death and life are in fact pitted against one another in this struggle, one would expect that these destructive forces would indeed be focused on the family, since there is no social institution more suited for shaping a culture of life than the family, the basic, vital unit of society.

This ought not to surprise us on either the natural or the supernatural level. On the supernatural level, through divine revelation, we know that marriage and the family are the direct creation of God Himself to serve His gift of life. "So God created man in his own image, in the image of God he created him; male and female He created them. And God blessed them, and God said to them, 'Be fruitful and multiply; and fill the earth and subdue it.'"[1]

The Objective Reality of Marriage
Denied in Today's Culture

On the natural level, through the *Atlantic Monthly*, the *Journal of Marriage and the Family,* and numerous psychological and sociological studies, we know that neglect of the family will bring disorder and devastation to individuals, families and societies. Despite the irrefutable sociological data, however, the cultural elite of our society simply fail to acknowledge the facts and to draw the appropriate conclusions from the data before them.

Judith Wallerstein, for example, has written on the devastating effects of divorce on children, even decades after the marital break-up has occurred.[2] Real healing seldom occurs; the psychic, the emotional wounds are always there in the children, even as they marry and begin their own families. But instead of drawing the sound conclusion that marital indissolubility best serves the interests of the children, she assumes the inevitability of divorce and calls for better ways to counsel children going through such difficulties.

The cultural elite will simply not accept that there is an objective reality to marriage and family by nature of God's creative design which simply cannot be changed at will. During the Clinton presidential inaugural parade there was a float given over to the theme of family. On it were a lesbian couple with a child, a male homosexual couple and a married heterosexual couple with their children. That float constituted a studied statement on the part of the Clinton Administration that a family is an arbitrary social construct which can be fashioned according to taste—and which ought to receive the recognition and sanction of the state.

The heart of the cultural problem surrounding marriage and the family today is that they are simply thought to be arbitrarily defined and constructed human institutions. This concept of the family was at the ideological heart of the Clinton delegations to both U.N. conferences which dealt with issues of the family, Cairo and Beijing.

Objective Nature of Marriage
Must be Socially Acknowledged

It is precisely the understanding of marriage and family as an arbitrary human construct which modern Popes have repudiated time and again. In *Casti Connubii* Pius XI wrote:

Let us . . . recall this immutable, inviolable, and fundamental truth: Matrimony was not instituted or reestablished by men but by God; not men, but God, the Author of nature, and Christ our Lord, the restorer of nature, provided marriage with its laws, confirmed and elevated it; and consequently those laws can in no way be subject to human wills or to any contrary pact made even by the contracting parties themselves. . . the perpetual indissolubility of the marriage bond, its unity and its stability, derive from God Himself.[3]

And when there is a departure from the created reality of marriage itself, disorder and death are introduced into society.

It is obvious that there can be no restoration of marriage and the family as powerful, positive social forces unless their divine origin and objective nature are acknowledged. This does not mean that there must be a broad social acceptance of the Catholic doctrine on the sacramentality of marriage. What will be required, however, is a social acceptance of marriage and the family as divinely created —and hence objective— institutions. Such an acceptance does not require faith. It requires a mind open to the truth of objective reality. Since marriage and family are objective realities accessible to the human mind, there will be social policies which quite obviously will contribute to their flourishing and others which will undermine them.

John Paul II asks: "What does the family as an institution expect from society?" And he answers:

> First of all, it expects a recognition of its identity and an acceptance of its status as a subject in society…Marriage, which undergirds the institution of the family, is consti-tuted by the covenant whereby 'a man and a woman establish between themselves a partnership of their whole life,' and which 'of its own very nature is ordered to the well-being of the spouses and to the procreation and upbringing of children.' Only such a union can be recognized and ratified as a 'marriage' in society. Other interpersonal unions which do not fulfil the above con-ditions cannot be recognized, despite certain growing trends which represent a serious threat to the future of the family and of society itself.[4]

Marriage and Family Institutionalize the "Life Drive"[5]

The family is the means which God Himself instituted to focus, channel and utilize the power for life which is given to humanity. Attempting to find other means of indulging the "life-drive" will mean not its fulfilment, not the realization of its inherent ends, but rather its disorder, its disorientation; it will mean the subversion and undermining of its inherent ends. In the chapter on temperance in his book *The Four Cardinal Virtues,*

Josef Pieper points out that the power for life becomes a drive for death when it is not properly ordered. When the life-drive, which is institutionalized in marriage, is not properly used, it becomes to one degree or another, death-dealing. As Pieper puts it: "Intemperance is self-destruction through the selfish degradation of the powers which aim at self-preservation."[6]

Medicine has shown the same phenomenon long observed by spiritual writers, i.e., a disordering of the fundamental drive to life renders it a drive to destruction and death. In his book *The Craving Brain,* Dr. Ronald Ruden points out that the impulses which drive destructive, addictive behaviors are the very ones which, when properly ordered and controlled, regulate the consumption of food, the protection of self and family, and the propagation of the species.[7] These drives are either appropriately ordered toward their inherent ends or they become forces for death. It is interesting that the ancient spiritual and pastoral handbooks would list sadism and masochism, not under the fifth commandment against killing, but rather under the sixth commandment against the misuse of our sexual appetite. St. Thomas points out that it is natural to man to love God more than himself.[8] Consequently, when one acts against the love of God one actually acts against oneself in a fundamentally destructive way since it is to act contrary to our nature.

The 1917 *Code of Canon Law* had used a definition of marriage which had been used in common theological treatises for centuries and which addressed matrimony's nurturing and life-giving character. "The primary end of marriage is the procreation and education of children; the secondary end is mutual support and a remedy for concupiscence."[9]

It is obvious that when couples recognize that marriage primarily serves the procreation and education of children, and they act accordingly, their marriage will contribute to the nurturing of a culture of life. Mutual support can also easily be seen as a life-nurturing end of marriage which will contribute to a culture of life. If the wife has the love and nurturing support of her husband, it is very unlikely she would ever be driven to abortion or would hold in low esteem the fruit of their mutual love.

However, even the end of marriage about which we hear little today, the *remedium concupiscentiae,* nurtures a culture of life. Marriage as the remedy for concupiscence is not to be understood simply as providing the legitimate context for the release of sexual tension. Much more profoundly it means the ordering of our basic drives for survival in ways which are fundamentally constructive rather than destructive. It means for husbands and fathers an ordering of their drives toward aggression and competition toward socially productive behavior. A study conducted at the University of Minnesota found that among men of comparable socio-economic and educational background, with comparable jobs, those who were married with a family were more productive than those who were single. That is an effect of the *remedium concupiscentiae.*

The Family Needs Other Social Institutions

But the family does not, indeed cannot, exist in isolation. As Pius XI pointed out in 1929 in *Divini Illius Magistri:* "In the first place comes the family, instituted directly by God for its peculiar purpose, the generation and formation of children; for this reason it has priority of nature and therefore of rights over civil society. *Nevertheless,* the family is an imperfect society, since it has not in itself all the means for its own complete development. . .the family. . .finds its own suitable temporal perfection precisely in civil society."

The family requires other social institutions to accomplish its own inherent ends. One striking characteristic of Catholic thought is its inner disposition toward integration, synthesis and harmony rather than division and atomization. The intense individualism of contemporary desacralized, indeed dechristianized, societies is a legacy of Protestantism and secularism, and the very antitheses of the Catholic temper. Despite the unparalleled importance placed on the institution of the family in Catholic doctrine, it is never set over against other social institutions but is seen as their complement and as contributing to their well-being.

In fact, it is recognized that the family cannot flourish without the institutions of academia and the Church and government. But today those institutions have failed the family in a most grievous fashion, for the simple reason, I believe, that these complementary social institutions have lost sight of what marriage and family are, in their most fundamental, objective constitution. Our Holy Father is profoundly aware of this. He asks in his *Letter to Families*, "Who can deny that our age is one marked by a great crisis, which appears above all as a profound 'crisis of truth'?" He goes on to insist, "Only if the truth about freedom and the communion of persons in marriage and the family can regain their splendor, will the building of the civilization of love truly begin and will it then be possible to speak concretely—as the Council did—about 'promoting the dignity of marriage and the family.'"[10]

Faced with this cultural uprooting, faced with the failure of complementary social institutions to provide appropriate support, families have been increasingly thrown back upon their own resources and led to forge alliances and cooperatives with other like-minded families. To look just briefly at the failure of these complementary institutions will illustrate the increasingly perilous position into which families have been placed.

Government

The government has failed families in a most egregious manner. Because of recent decisions of courts and legislatures the protection of the state has been withdrawn from vulnerable children in their mothers' wombs, the very heart of what ought to constitute familial integrity and society's hope for the future.

Roe v. Wade was a blow struck against the family as much as it was a blow struck against innocent, unborn human life. The State has become one of the principal molders of the culture of death.

The Supreme Court decision *Planned Parenthood v. Danforth* in 1976 was another wedge driven between husband and wife, father and child, when it decreed that a father could not intervene to save his unborn child if the mother was intent upon killing it. The legislature of Missouri, in an attempt to restrict the growing practice of abortion in the wake of *Roe v. Wade*, had required the consent of the husband before the child could be killed by the mother and the abortion. (Of course there is no *moral* legitimacy to the father consenting to the abortion but Roe v. Wade severely limited the safeguards for the unborn child which could legally put in place by the State.) However, for Planned Parenthood even this proved too much of a restraint on the unbridled will of the mother do do whatever she wanted. The Supreme Court wrote in that decision that "the State may not constitutionally require the consent of the spouse . . . since it [the State] cannot delegate to a spouse a veto power which the State itself is absolutely and totally prohibited from exercising."

In this decision there is a denial that the husband has any *natural* right with regard to his wife and child, specifically a right, and indeed a corresponding obligation, to try to protect his child from assault. There is also the implication in that decision that it is the thinking of the Court that it is the State which delegates rights to the spouses rather than the state recognizing that the rights and obligations of husbands and wives, mothers and fathers, are theirs by nature upon having entered into the relationship of marriage; they are not granted by the State.

It is an individualist and materialist ideology which now drives family policy in the United States. For the first time in history, children have "divorced" their natural parents in two celebrated court cases. Many advocates of children's rights in the United States believe that the interests of children can be advanced only if they are viewed as isolated, autonomous individuals with no natural moral ties to their biological parents. This individualist and materialist ideology can also be seen in the development of divorce law in the United States, which claims marriage as another victim of the culture of death. More than 50% of marriages in the United States end in divorce. Some sociologists maintain that the probability of a first marriage being terminated is now as high as 60%. This is now often accomplished through a procedure known as "no-fault" divorce.

Most no-fault divorce laws are based upon such materialistic presuppositions that what is divided is only tangible property. However, the husband has often accumulated a non-tangible type of property over the years, and often with the help of this wife: a law degree, a medical license, business contacts. These obviously cannot be divided and remain the "property" of the man. What is happening in the United States is an attempt to deal with marriage solely in quantifiable terms.

The effects of supposedly treating men and women as equal entities with claims to equal amounts of property can easily be measured. Studies have shown that the standard of living of divorced women and their children drops 73% in the first year after divorce, while the standard of living of the divorced men *increases 42%*. Also as no-fault, no-consent divorce laws were being enacted no consideration was given to the fact that divorcing couples often have so little money that they have to sell their home to bring about an equal division of marital property. This loss of the family home and the uprooting from the familiar neighborhood invariably contribute to the insecurity and trauma experienced by children who suffer through the divorce of their parents. As Leo XIII wrote "Truly it is hardly possible to describe how great are the evils that flow from divorce." Those words were spoken well over a hundred years ago. Yet despite sociological findings, let aside papal teaching, we are far from acknowledging in our public policy, the absolutely essential role of the intact family for societal flourishing.

Virtually everyone agrees that teenage sexual activity and drug use are a scourge in modern society, ruining lives and costing billions in tax dollars. Family disintegration contributes significantly to these problems. Yet the Catholic Church is virtually a lone voice today insisting on marital indissolubility.

Emily Rosenbaum of Columbia University and Denise B. Kandel of Columbia and the New York State Psychiatric Institute wrote on drug abuse and teenage sexual activity. "Several studies support the importance of family structure on precocious sexual activity. The likelihood of early sex is consistently higher among adolescents living in nonintact than in an intact family. . . Furthermore, the emotional turmoil of a divorce or separation may prompt the teenager to seek comfort outside the home."[11] In other words, it would seem that if the State wanted to reduce teenage sexual promiscuity and the accompanying threats of illegitimate children or the dangers of abortion or the spread of AIDS it would do all in its power to strengthen families rather than undermining them through no-fault divorce.

Dr. Thomas Ewin Smith of the University of South Carolina did an extensive survey of the relevant literature and wrote: "There is considerable evidence . . . that lower academic achievement of children and adolescents is related to parental divorce . . . [M]ajor reviews of relevant research . . . have found that children from two-parent families have higher measured mental aptitude, academic achievement, and school grades than those from one-parent families . . . being in a one-parent family significantly reduced the reading and mathematics achievement scores of both white and black elementary school students."[12]

The State has failed our families and through its virtual monopoly on education in the United States has undermined the role of parents as the primary educators of their children. All of the forces contributing to the culture of death and impeding the development of the culture of life are of course interrelated.

The Schools

Our schools have failed the family. The primary end of education is the teaching of virtue. The imparting of information is and must be secondary to the shaping of character. Yet most of our schools today tell us that the imparting of virtue is the one thing which they cannot do. There is no longer a shared moral vision in society, we are told. There is no way of determining "whose" morality should be taught. As a result we have "value free" education, and more mindlessly, "value free" sex education. Consequently, our children are disoriented, disarmed. Among school children suicide, drug use, and sexual activity are at some of the highest levels ever in the United States.

The schools are certainly one place where our children should feel safe. Yet a 1994 report by the National School Boards of America showed that in the preceding five years violence had increased in 82 percent of the nation's schools. The Institute for Social Research looked to statistics from the Justice Department and found that 91.6 perent of public high school seniors worry about crime and violence. And in 1994 a Gallup poll found that in the preceding year one teen in five had a friend who was attacked by someone who had a knife or gun; 7 percent had themselves been assaulted and 14 percent had been the victims of vandalism.[13]

In our great nation, even illiteracy has become a problem. The U. S. Chamber of Commerce estimates that functional illiteracy costs U.S. business $300 billion annually in lost productivity.[14] The cost to self esteem and personal enrichment is of course incalculable.

Finally, through sex education programs and the distribution of contraceptives the schools are significantly contributing to the spread of the culture of death. Any study which I have ever read has shown a positive correlation between school sex education and contraceptive distribution programs and an increase in unwanted pregnancies, which of course leads to a further breakdown of the family structure and most regrettably to destructive acts of abortion and infanticide.

The Churches Have Failed the Family

Even the churches have failed the family. There is hardly a need to reflect on the moral confusion to be found today in the main line Protestant churches. But even those who work within the bureaucracies of the Catholic Church have failed the family in many ways. Marriage tribunals have often spread confusion about the indissoluble character of marriage. The head of one tribunal told me he thought that most marriages in his diocese were probably null. With such thinking at the head of a tribunal how will the judges be approaching the sacramental reality of marriage? And what does such a thought say about that tribunal judge's understanding of the working of God's grace in effecting, in bringing about, sacramental realities? Theologians have taught that the goodness and grace of God is such that a sacrament is brought about even with a minimum of intentionality and consent on the part of the baptized parties who are being married.

Every theologian who has continued in his or her academic post at a Catholic institution or who has worked in an "office of marriage and family" while repudiating the Church's teaching on contraception has struck a blow at the foundation of sound and healthy marriages by striking a blow at marital chastity. And those who would permit those theologians and bureaucrats to remain in their positions have failed Catholic families, have failed non-Catholic families and have in their own way contributed to the break down of the family and hence the social order in the United States.

It is scandalous the extent to which many Christian bodies have acquiesced in the area of divorce and remarriage, abortion, euthanasia and homosexual advocacy. Episcopalian bishops ordain open, active homosexuals to the ministry. One of the

most effective spokesmen for and ardent supporters of physician-assisted suicide is an ordained Unitarian minister. A Catholic
bishop wears sacred vestments adorned with homosexual insig-
nia and another offers support to homosexual militants by
spending time with them in Cape Town at their haunts. The
churches, too, have undermined the family's role as a bulwark
against the culture of death because many of their leaders have
become practical atheists. That is, even though they may acknowledge the existence of God, they fail to see the implications
of such a belief in the realm of moral action.

Families Respond

We have considered briefly some of the social and cultural
influences which have unleashed the forces of death against the
family because it is these we must work to alter. Catholic
families and the Church must devise strategies to reclaim these
complementary social institutions so that they once again serve
families and the common good.

The family, the most basic cell of both political society and
the supernatural society of the Church, is essential to the
building up of a culture of life. The Civilization of Love
cannot be realized without strong, vibrant, healthy, flourishing
families.

The family has been forced increasingly to fall back upon its
own resources. But that should not be discouraging in the least,
since even the family's natural resources are, after all, of divine
origin.

One of the most critical institutions which the family has at
its disposal to contribute to a culture of life is clearly the school.
But the family must be allowed to exert its full influence. One of
the most pervasive and cruel injustices in the United States is the
virtual monopoly of the government on education. It is patently
unjust that parents have to pay to support two school systems if
they want their children to receive a Catholic education.

One of the most critically important current social initiatives to which Catholic parents should be uncompromisingly committed is school choice. But in the interim, until that battle is won, parents in unprecedented numbers have begun educating their children at home. Estimates are that seven hundred thousand to one million children are now being taught at home. The home school movement shows the extent to which parents see the current institutions of academia as no longer being a force for good.

One of the most useful tools available today to parents home schooling their children—or even helping their children who are in private or public schools—is the Internet. The explosion of pornography on the Internet is absolutely deplorable but the capacity of this technology to be of help to parents doing education at home is extraordinary. Home schoolers have an incredible array of websites. One can go on the Internet and find out what the laws are in every state of the union regarding home schooling.

If parents are having difficulty teaching physics to their children, for example, they can find physicists on the Internet who are deeply committed to home schooling, to Christian education. and to our values who are willing to offer their services. Other Internet sites offer model curricula. It is a great tool.

Parents *must* take the education of their children into their own hands. The schools have largely failed us, and so we must be very careful about where we place our children. We must attempt to place them in schools which impart the truth about marriage and family, about science and religion, about morality and public order. Sometimes it will be necessary to send our children to public schools because of the expense of the Catholic school or because the public school would not pose as much a moral danger as some Catholic schools. But whether our children are in public or Catholic schools their education and formation occur mostly at home.

With proper training and education from the parents, and armed with their own moral beliefs, our children can be effective counter-influences to the culture of death. One of my daughters was in a public school and had to make a presentation on contraception which she did on the dangers to the health and even the life of women who use the intra-uterine device. And since she used scientific data, some of it gathered by Planned Parenthood itself, the teacher was unable to refute anything she presented.

Another of our children in a public school had to write a persuasive essay on some contemporary controversy. Our son chose abortion. The class had just finished studying the *Merchant of Venice*. In the course of my son's essay, he placed the words of the Jew Shylock into the mouth of an unborn child: "If you prick us, do we not bleed? If you tickle us, do we not laugh? If you poison us, do we not die?"[15]

The teacher, who was pro-abortion, covered his paper with her commentary in red ink trying to refute his arguments. But she gave him an "A" for writing a persuasive essay and admitted to having been stunned by the Shakespearean quote in the mouth of an unborn child.

We do not have to wait until we have won on the issue of school choice for our children to receive a proper education in morality. It must be done at home, and our children can immediately begin permeating society and working toward the building of the Culture of Life.

The Politics of the Family

The family must also bring great pressure to bear on the State. The so-called politics of the family has been a most welcome development in recent years. Those family advocacy groups which have been most vigilant and most effective, in my opinion, such as Focus on the Family, the Family Research Council and the Heritage Foundation, have been of Protestant inspiration to a large extent. It has been very gratifying to see the extent to which Catholics have been welcomed into and have participated very significantly in these organizations.

The truth of the matter is that the doctrinal positions of the Catholic church are more in accord with the political programs of any of these Protestant-inspired organizations than the theologies of those Protestant churches themselves. It is my opinion that we should welcome and encourage collaboration with these groups because I believe they will help significantly in building up a Culture of Life. However the family has at its disposal not only its own natural resources of blood, kinship, loyalty, and political advocacy, but most importantly supernatural resources of sanctifying grace, sacramental grace, and the prayers of the saints triumphant in heaven and the choirs of angels and archangels. Catholics are frankly derelict if they do not avail themselves of all these resources.

Nothing is more important for members of Catholic families trying to forge a Culture of Life, than for them to be in a state of grace. The Blessed Jose Maria Escriva compared trying to accomplish good works without grace to a seamstress trying to sew up a dress with a needle but no thread. Our efforts may be there, they may even be frenetic, but ultimately they will be of no good. There will be no Culture of Life without God's grace.

Everything must be done to strengthen the family, naturally and supernaturally. But when we speak in terms of political strategies to build a culture of life, we have to look to the long term. There must be the struggle for parents to regain control of their children's education, to fight to obtain tax relief for families, and the countless battles which must be waged against pornography and abortion. We must also fight against the social acceptance and the availability of contraception. Regrettably these are not victories which we can hope to obtain in the near future; most will not be realized in our lifetime. But there are certain actions which must be taken now, which cannot wait.

There are initiatives which we can undertake within the hour. We must immediately begin doing what can be done in our own lives, and in our own interpersonal relationships within the family. Otherwise any victory which we may win through the politics of the family will be a Pyrrhic victory which will not ultimately serve the individuals for whom we wage the struggle. We do not work for some abstraction known as the family. We do not pretend we will be able to build some utopian culture of life. I speak personally here, but what I say is applicable to anyone. I do not work long hours and spend painful periods of time away from my home because I hope to contribute to some abstraction such as social justice, or because I want to help humanity, or even because I want to strengthen the institution of "the family". I do it for Martha, Clare, Sophia, Justin, Matthew, Rebecca, Katherine, Lydia, Mary, Stephen, and Joe.

The old adage reminds us that charity begins at home. The Epistle of John asks how we can love God, whom we have not seen, if we cannot love our brother, whom we have seen,. How can I love my fellow citizens in this nation, or the world, if I do not love my children, my wife, my sisters and brothers, my parents-in-law. John Paul II has stressed this need for concrete individualized love repeatedly in his pontificate. In his *Letter to Families*, the Holy Father writes, "Man is created not only as an individual who is part of the multitude of humanity, but rather as *this* individual. God the creator calls him into existence for himself; 'this man' has in every instance the right to fulfill himself on the basis of his humanity. It is precisely this dignity which establishes a person's place among others, and above all in the family. The family is, indeed, more than any other human reality, THE place where an individual can exist 'for himself', through the sincere gift of self. This is why it remains a social institution which neither can nor should be replaced; it is the sanctuary of life."

Each individual within the family, by name, must be loved, and cherished, and served because we were saved by an individual with a name, Jesus; who was nurtured by loving parents with names, Mary and Joseph.

At the most intimate core of the life of families must be the imitation of Jesus Christ. In our families we must live out the life of the Son who came to do not His own will but the will of the Father. Within our families we must live out the life of the Lamb offered in sacrifice, of the Bridegroom who offered up His life for His Bride. We must discover Jesus and His will in Sacred Scripture and live it out in imitation of Him.

If the family is to become once again a positive force for the transformation of our society into a culture of life, it must begin with the spouses' unqualified surrender to one another and together to their children.

Father Walter Farrell, a commentator on St. Thomas, pointed out that children, in the thought of St. Thomas, come under the heading of compensations within marriage. But the compensations are seen in their drawing forth sacrifice from their parents. "For the child is a perfect expression of love; here is a union that is an embodiment of mother and father; a surrender, for here is a master of them both; a consecration, for here is one that lifts them both to heroic heights of sacrifice."[16]

If we are to build the culture of life through the family then husbands and wives must live together chastely, never using one another as merely an object of physical pleasure. To love one's spouse but not to love the fertility of one's spouse is ultimately not to love one's spouse fully. If for some serious reason a couple should avoid having a child at a given time, spouses respect and love one another's fertility by not assaulting their respective fruitfulness by contraceptive acts. They simply avoid conjugal relations at a time when their fertility would most likely engender a new life. They respect, honor and love the fertility of the other by not acting against it, and most significantly, by not acting against the procreative end which would be inherent in the act of fruitfulness should they choose to engage in it.

It is not the artificiality of contraception which renders it immoral but rather the unreasonable choice of acting specifically against the procreative good which would be inherent within the act of fertility in which a couple would choose to engage. Contraception always involves an act other than the marital act, and that other act has no end, no purpose, other than to stifle the procreative meaning of the act.

In his *Letter to Families*, Pope John Paul speaks of the "civilization of love" and "responsible fatherhood and motherhood" as "two closely related questions." At the very heart of the Pope's discussion of the building up of a *civilization* of love, he raises the intensely *personal* question of contraception. John Paul II sees the link between marital chastity and life, marital unchastity and death. So did St. Augustine in the fifth century. His words have a distressing contemporaneity to them.

[The licentious cruelty of the marital couple] or their cruel licentiousness, sometimes goes to such lengths as to procure sterilizing poisons, and if these are unavailing, in some way to stifle within the womb and eject the fetus that has been conceived. They want their offspring to die before it comes to life, or, if it is already living in the womb, to perish before it is born. Surely, if they are both of such a mind, they do not deserve the name of husband and wife; and if they have been of such mind from the beginning, it was not for wedlock but for fornication that they became united. If they are not both of such a mind, then I will venture to say that either the woman is the mere mistress of the husband or the man is the paramour of the wife.[17]

Only within the context of sacrificial love manifested in Christ can the Church's teaching on marriage and the family be understood and its apostolate to modern society be carried out. The members of a family give themselves in surrender to one another and the fruit of that surrender is life. Only when the family is strong can it be of service to society at large. It will be strong only when it is patterned after the life and the death of Jesus Christ.

Granting the value of organizations and voluntary associations and political action groups in transforming modern society, absolutely nothing can replace the witness of one family to another. Catholic families must cultivate friendships. They should organize occasions to get together with other families. They should arrange to have their children socialize with children from other Catholic families so that, God willing, they will someday form new strong Catholic families of their own.

This personal, one-on-one apostolate on the part of families for the building of a culture of life cannot be stressed too much. The dreadful social disorder we see around us today did not occur overnight and it cannot be remedied overnight. And families must be the primary means for remedying today's disorders.

The Second Vatican Council addressed this reality in its *Decree on the Apostolate of Lay People*: "Christian couples are, for each other, for their children and for their relatives, cooperators of grace and witnesses of the faith. They are the first to pass on the faith to their children and to educate them in it. By word and example they form them to a Christian and apostolic life."[18] But such a life does not stay contained in the family. We know that it is of the nature of goodness to diffuse itself, to spread out. The decree goes on: "The mission of being the primary vital cell of society has been given to the family by God Himself."[19] It is veritably the task of the Catholic family to save society.

It is because of the primary, essential and vital importance of the family, that we lay people find there our most important task in bringing about the culture of life. Families most effectively reach out to families in what the Council called the "apostolate of like to like".

The apostolate in one's social environment endeavors to infuse the Christian spirit into the mentality and behavior, laws and structures of the community in which one lives. To such a degree is it the special work and responsibility of lay people, that no one else can ever properly supply for them. In this area laymen can conduct the apostolate of like to like.[20]

As families carry out their apostolate they must live the life of God. Family life is to be patterned after the Trinitarian life of love, and no one exemplifies this for us better than the most Holy Mother of God. As we face the dangers posed by the culture of death we turn to her who bore the One who called Himself "the Life".

Notes

1. Genesis 1: 27-28

2. Judith Wallertstein with Dr. Joan Kelly, *Surviving the Breakup: How Children and Parents Cope with Divorce* (Basic Books, 1980), which grew out of the original California *Children of Divorce Study* begun in 1971. *Second Chances: Men, Women and Children a Decade After Divorce* (Ticknor& Fields, New York, 1989), co-authored with Sandra Blakeslee), comprises the 10- and 15-year follow-up reports on her longitudinal study and is a compendium of her clinical observations.

3. Pius XI, *Casti Connubii*, 1930.

4. John Paul II, *Letter to Families for the Year of the Family*, February 2, 1994.

5. I am using "Life Drive" to refer to what has traditionally been termed the "concupiscible appetite".

6. Josef Pieper, *Four Cardinal Virtues* (South Bend, 1954), p. 148.

7. Ronald A. Ruden, M.D., Ph.D. with Marcia Byalick, *The Craving Brain* (New York: Harper Collins, 1997). See also Jo Durden-Smith and Diane Desimone, *Sex and the Brain* (New York: Arbor House, 1983).

8. St. Thomas Aquinas, *Summa Theologica*, 2a2ae, Q. 26, Art. 3.

9. "Matrimonii finis primarius est procreatio atque educatio prolis; secundarius mutuum adjutorium et remedium concupiscentiae." *Codex Iuris Canonici* (New York: P.J. Kennedy & Sons, 1918), Canon 1013.

10. *Letter*, 13. The conciliar quotation is from *Gaudium et Spes*, 47.

11. Emily Rosenbaum and Denise B. Kandel. "Early Onset of Adolescent Sexual Behavior and Drug Involvement". *Journal of Marriage and the Family*, 52:3 (August 1990), p. 784.

12. Thomas Ewin Smith. "Parental Separation and the Academic Self-Concepts of Adolescents: An Effort to Solve the Puzzle of Separation Effects". Journal of Marriage and the Family, 52:1 (February 1990), pp. 107-108.

13. "Violence and Teens in the Home and in the Schools in the 1990's," The George H. Gallup International Institute, March 10, 1994.

14. Tim Sullivan, "Has School Reform Flunked?" *The World and I*, September 1996, p. 61.

15. William Shakespeare, *The Merchant of Venice*, Act 3, Scene 1.

16. Walter Farrell, O.P., *Commentary on the Summa, Volume 4*, p. 408.

17. *De nuptiis et concupiscentiae*, 15.15.

18. *Decree on the Apostolate of Lay People (Apostolicam Actuositatem)*, 11.

19. *Decree on the Apostolate of Lay People*, 22.

20. *Decree on the Apostolate of Lay Persons*, 13.

Building the Culture of Life through the Family: A Response

Mary Ellen Bork

Dr. Haas's excellent presentation shows us once again the wisdom of Catholic teaching on the family in its natural and supernatural dimensions in building the culture of life. The God-given life-affirming role of the family and the view of life rooted in Biblical teaching are not supported by a post-Christian culture and its virulent hostility to religion and We are at a cultural turning point when the family, the institution that shapes the culture, is denied by the elites to even exist as an objective reality, and the desires of the individual take precedence over the family. With Jeremiah we can lament that things look very bleak indeed and we look to God to restore the land.

The extent to which our culture is undermining family life is unprecedented in Western history. In every area of life from the music and films of popular culture to social welfare policy the traditional understanding of the family as a close-knit hierarchical group of mother, father and children is replaced by the notion of "families"—any group of individuals who want to live together, each with their own rights. The idea of marriage and family as a desirable norm of society is challenged by elite groups who understand marriage as personal fulfillment, that is, as long as it lasts. As the cultural ground shifts towards the culture of death, the question of whether the direction can be changed back to firmer ground that is traditional and moral is hard to answer. (I am not a pessimist but I have been tutored by the author of *Slouching Towards Gomorrah* on just how far gone the situation is.)

I agree with Dr. Haas that the heart of the problem is that marriage and family are seen as institutions that can be arbitrarily defined. The centuries old understanding of the family has been dissolved under the influence of radical feminism, the rise of radical individualism, and the sexual revolution of the 60's, and I would add, nihilism. Gender feminism, which has replaced equality feminism, is, I think, the most dangerous long-term destructive influence on the family. Feminists represent the vangard of what John Paul II calls the aggressive forces of the "anti-civilization."

Gender feminists insist that women are oppressed by men and are victims of the order created by males, whether white, black or yellow, in society and in the church. In their hostility to that order they are promoting an understanding of freedom as individualism, gender as a social construct, and power as necessary to their self-fulfilment. They want nothing less than to change the social order to reflect a basically nihilistic understanding of life with no reference to God. If they do refer to God or goddess it is a gnostic new-age myth they have in mind. The most radical ones speak of marriage as rape and pregnancy as the presence of an invader in the body of a woman who can legally be fended off.[1] Family or motherhood or pregnancy are all reduced to options which a woman can choose, not part of an ordered vision of life in which the woman has the special role of giving the first home to the child in her own body, in her womb. Children are seen as burdens, expensive and time-consuming. Unlike Father Farrell's view that "the child is a perfect expression of love; (here is) a union that is an embodiment of mother and father; a surrender, for here is a master of them both; a consecration, for here is one that lifts them both to heroic heights of sacrifice."[2] Feminists deny the truth of women's complementary relationship with man and cultivate this dangerous myth that gender is a malleable concept, a social construct, not rooted in sexuality, in other words, gender is whatever they say it is. This approach is reflected in the document from the U.N. Beijing conference on Women in which the word family never is used, members belong to "households" and the word "mother" is replaced by "caregiver."

Along with the feminist agenda elements of family culture are being undermined by those who assume that institutions can rear children better than parents. The role of parents as the primary teachers and nurturers of children tends to be undermined by these same influences. That is the message of books like Hilary Clinton's *It Takes a Village* and Sylvia Hewlett's *When the Bough Breaks*. Parents are no longer seen as responsible sources of wisdom. They are pariahs who misuse their authority over their children and need the wisdom of educational and child welfare experts to help them with a job they are not trained for. They often feel isolated because they lack a community supportive of the moral virtues they want to teach their children. Programs offered by family welfare services often confuse parents by making destructive interventions in family lives. Parents have to deal with schools that suggest that their children report on parents who spank, and those that send children home with lists of their rights vis à vis their parents. Some parents can have their children taken away to foster homes over minor matters that are reported by determined bureaucrats.

Parents have to contend with schools offering many programs disruptive of family culture. There are many "life skills" courses that openly challenge the values parents teach at home. Sex ed is presented to children as young as six. A recent *National Review* cartoon showed the intrusiveness of this culture. Two young children are playing. One says, "I found a condom on the patio." The other child says, "What is a patio?"[3]

The legal culture has failed parents in divorce law, adoption and custody fights as well as in their everyday exercise of authority over their children. The trend against parental authority is illustrated by a 1985 case in New York. A fifteen-year-old girl ran away from home because her mother forbade her to pursue a relationship with a twenty-one-year-old lesbian. The mother requested the court to order the girl home identifying her as a person in need of supervision. The judge refused the request claiming that "the mother's effort to place limits on her child's adolescent sexual involvement overstepped her legal competence as the child's protector. The child, insisted the judge, had the 'right' to 'sexual self-determination.' He advised both mother and daughter, whom he effectively regarded as equals before the court, to "reconcile their differences within the framework of this decision."[4] Professor Mary Ann Glendon has described the legal system as increasingly blind to the importance of strong family ties as a prerequisite for a healthy society. "In upholding individual "self-sufficiency as an ideal," in disparaging the natural "intersubjectivity" of family relationships, and in encouraging state and bureaucratic intervention in family life, the law, she says, treats the family as if it were an antisocial force—a force engaged in fostering dependency and isolating individuals from the larger social environment."[5] Families are the greatest pro-social force forming attitudes in children that enable them to interact with other persons and institutions. Recent laws regarding divorce and custody of children are based on a notion of the family as a loose association of individuals with little regard for the strong emotional bonds among the members. There is little recognition that families need nurturing as much as they need rights.

Dr. Haas has indicated the direction of our response to this cultural assault on the family: reevangelization about the identity of the family and its esteemed role; spiritual formation in the attitudes of the heart of Christ, prayer, self-sacrifice, and fidelity; and public Catholicism which defends and articulates the teachings of the Church in the public square and also joins with others in active advocacy of the new familism and the debate over parental rights. The new familism is the result of baby boomers discovering parenthood and represents a philosophical shift that puts them at odds with the intellectual elites. "More and more parents of young children are realizing that work-life and family-life conflict, that time is scarcer than money, and that time and attention are the chief currencies of family life."[6] They object to the idea that caretakers can raise children as well as they can and are finding inventive ways of combining work and family life.

Pope John Paul II has laid the intellectual and theological groundwork for the formation of a holy laity to take a new role in the transformation of culture on behalf of the flourishing of families. Dr. Haas pointed out that the nature of Catholic thought leads to integration and synthesis. This quality should be effective in the work of reevangelizing a society in which "the center cannot hold" and people have lost the sense of meaning. Many Catholics identify Catholic social teaching with a few issues such as the minimum wage, the death penalty, and abortion and are unaware of its larger vision of life. They need a more systematic teaching on the social principles of Catholic life, the dignity of the human person, the family as a community of love, the principle of subsidiarity, provided by the *Catechism* and the clear teachings of Pope John Paul II. This teaching should be directly related to their everyday life so it is not seen as an abstraction but as guidelines for their life in the world. Transformed by God's grace and a holy life, they are to transform the culture. Through parishes and lay organizations this teaching can be given, must be given. The laity need a fresh understanding of the eternal significance of their roles as responsible fathers and mothers. This should be a constant focus of preaching at Sunday Mass as well as the program of lay organizations.

Spiritual formation will be a part of the experience of family life in the "domestic church". Children learn from the example of parents who pray, who continue to cultivate virtue in their adult life and exercise discernment in dealing with the vicissitudes of a hostile culture. Parents and children will be sustained by the Holy Spirit as they grow together in a communion of persons. They are formed by the Church and in the Church through its liturgy and sacraments into the body of Christ. The Christian attitude of self-sacrifice modeled on the life of Jesus is at the heart of a happy family life. This is also the Catholic answer to individualism, to become one with Christ. C.S. Lewis says we are like "marble waiting to be shaped, metal waiting to be run into a mould."[7] Our value is not in our own individuality but in our receiving value from God. Through grace God is forming us in Christ. We are becoming new creatures who will be fully ourselves in Heaven. The sacraments open us up to the life of God. New age religion closes in on the self as god. The increase in devotion to the Eucharist in many parts is a sign of people turning back to God. The Church's fidelity to orthodox teaching is the most important contribution to supporting families in the cultural battle. Spiritual formation must lead us beyond being pious to a unified life inspired by faith that is fully embraced, entirely thought out and faithfully lived.[8]

Dr. Haas included some reflections on his own experience in the course of his talk. That may seem a minor point but by doing so he illustrated the importance of recognizing the ways in which our everyday experience incarnates our views of family. Sharing these experiences is part of the pedagogy that will be most instructive to the young and the unchurched, and the rechurched.

The third area of supporting families is through public Catholicism, entering the public debates on issues affecting the family and having the courage to be pummelled and sometimes be victorious. Since almost every issue affecting families has become politicized there is no excuse for the laity to not find an issue of interest. Besides advocacy for school choice we need to support the new familism and build a network that can translate good ideas into reality.

Many of the attacks on the family are not just the result of disagreements about ways to approach problems but are coordinated agendas by well-funded groups. Parents realize they need to take steps to separate themselves from the culture of death and take new initiatives that are countercultural and significant. This is a new more active role for many parents and they need the support of the Church and of other laity to be successful. One of the most significant steps has been the search for alternative schooling and the home school movement. There are now about one million parents who home school and with great success. In the 1970's they numbered 12,500. Parent-run advocacy groups speak out on controversial school policies such as "outcome based education," school choice, and national testing. Informal support groups for women as well as organized ones are flourishing. National groups like Promise Keepers and the National Fatherhood Initiative are helping men recover from the feminist and secular assault and affirm their roles as fathers and husbands. The National Organization for Women has targeted Promise Keepers for presenting a stereotype of traditional marriage and man's role as controlling the household. Promise Keepers' message encourages responsible fatherhood, commitment to purity, fidelity in marriage and faith in God, a message that most women celebrate and that most poor communities welcome. Women do not fear Promise Keepers but NOW does because it denies their agenda.

In the face of coordinated attacks on the family, Catholics need the strength that comes from a deeper grasp of the elements of Catholic family life as well as a coordinated response that comes from families themselves. The harmful "ideologies...that make the very springs of life dry up" are failing those who promote them.[9] Our witness to the order created by God which joins man and woman in marriage and creates the community of persons in the family is itself the culture of life which will attract those who have been beguiled by myths. We are living at a time when we realize that all of our choices for truth and life whether large or small are significant because they hold back for one more day the encroaching culture of death. Like Mother Teresa's example, the more concrete, hands-on, and visible our charity the more even the most hardened hearts may be touched to respond and the hearts of fathers will be turned back to their children and the land will be restored.

Notes

1. Eileen L. McDonagh, *Breaking the Abortion Deadlock: From Choice to Consent*, Oxford University Press, 1996.

2. John Hass, "Building the Culture of Life Through the Family", paper given at Fellowship of Catholic Scholars meeting, Washington, D.C., September 20, 1997, p.21.

3. National Review, September 15, 1997, vol. XLIX, no. 17, p.54.

4. Dana Mack, *The Assault on Parenthood: How Our Culture Undermines the Family*, Simon and Schuster, 1997, p. 94.

5. Dana Mack, p. 105.

6. Mack, p. 265.

7. C.S. Lewis, "Membership" in *The Weight of Glory*, Macmillan Publishing Company, 1980.

8. John Paul II, *Christifidelis Laici*, 1988, p.178.

9. *Christifidelis Laici*, p.117.

PART V

BUILDING THE CULTURE OF LIFE THROUGH LAW

Building the Culture of Life Through Law

Bernard Dobranski
The Catholic University of America
Washington, D.C.

When Carl Anderson asked me to speak at this year's convention on this topic, I was not sure I wanted to accept. The suggested topic—*Building a Culture of Life Through the Law* —was not one that I was particularly keen on tackling. Not because I—a law professor and a Catholic—do not care about the law and how it relates to issues of life. But because I do care and because, quite frankly, the law—particularly the law in the sense of that promulgated by the United States Supreme Court– has been the major force in creating and maintaining what Pope John Paul II has so correctly labeled the "culture of death". My reluctance thus was due to a pessimism about the likelihood of the law being useful at all in building a "culture of life," given that it has been a major influence in destroying respect for life.

The more I reflected on the topic, however, the more I became convinced that there were some useful things to be said and that there are some reasons to be optimistic about restoring a culture of life through the law.

Let me now offer you my reflections on this issue—not in a definitive or scholarly fashion—but in a conversational mode. My point is simply this: Yes, there is reason for optimism, at least a cautious, guarded optimism, that we can transform our culture back to one of respect for life through the law. The road that needs to be taken to affect this transformation, however, is a perilous one with many roadblocks, potholes, antagonistic travelers going in other directions and seeking to knock us off the road or deny us access to the road, and heavy tolls to be paid along the way. But it is a road well worth traveling, for at the end, if we reach the end successfully, we will have created a dramatic transformation in the law and the culture.

Let me tell you how I plan to proceed. I will start with a few brief comments about what I mean by culture, how the culture affects the law, and how the law, in turn, affects culture; I will then speak briefly to the point obvious to all—that there is an interaction between the culture and law that has led to the "culture of death". From there, I will speak about the recent decisions by the U.S. Supreme Court in the assisted suicide cases and what they portend—the challenges and problems they present and the opportunities and openings they create which give reason to believe that a restored culture of life through the law is possible.

When I use the term "culture", I am referring to both the so called "popular" culture and to the "elite" culture, and to the institutions through which they are communicated—television, both network and cable; movies; the popular newspapers and magazines like the NY Times, the Washington Post, Time, Newsweek and People; and our academic institutions.

The point that the culture can and does affect the law seems obvious. When Peter Finley Dunne's famous Mr. Dooley remarked that the Supreme Court followed the election returns, he was talking, in a sense, to the Court following the culture. Justice Oliver Wendell Holmes, certainly a member of the cultural elite, was fond of observing that the Supreme Court responds to the "felt necessities of the times". Justice Brennan's "evolving constitution" or his call to read the Constitution as a twentieth century American is nothing more than an appeal to the

142

influence of the culture, or at least to his view of what the culture desires. The so-called "Greenhouse" effect (that is the good opinion of the New York Times, through its Supreme Court reporter Linda Greenhouse) and its apparent impact on the voting behavior of certain justices is another example of the culture affecting law.

There are also various other ways the culture subtly influences how we, and ultimately how judges, think about certain issues. One way is to create an atmosphere that suggests certain values are paramount or particularly important. For example, the media may skew the arguments by insisting on a vocabulary of "choice" or of "death with dignity" or by marginalizing or refusing to let certain views be heard. These efforts, as minor as they appear, are nonetheless very significant in terms of affecting how we think about these issues, and this, in turn, affects how judges think about them. Many more examples could be given, but they are hardly necessary because the point is obvious. The culture we live in affects the way judges think about the law and, ultimately, the law itself. As Jude Dougherty, the distinguished Dean of The Catholic University of America's School of Philosophy has noted:

> The Supreme Court in recent decades has allocated to itself the role of moral arbiter for the nation, and in that activist role it has reflected not so much the traditions of the people as a whole, but the perceptions of an intellectual elite.

The influence, of course, is not all in one direction. Not only does the culture affect the law, but the law influences, shapes, directs, and fashions the culture. It, too, serves as a catalyst. In fact, the two—law and culture—are inextricably intertwined. In this regard, I ask you to think for a moment what the culture would be like if the Supreme Court had upheld prayer in schools, had found no constitutional right to abortion, had decided

143

pornography and obscenity could be controlled by communities in meaningful way, and had found no penumbras emanating from anywhere in the constitution. I recognize, of course, that a culture more respectful of life would not have been inevitable, even with more favorable decisions in these matters. It may well have been the case that other cultural forces would have over-whelmed the effects of even favorable decisions, and the culture today might not be significantly different, even with a different set of judicial results. But I do not believe that that would have been the case. Rather, I am convinced that had our Supreme Court, and our state courts as well, handled these fundamental issues in a different way, our society would be much different and much better, particularly as it relates to the issues of life, religion, values and the family. I also do not mean to suggest that the courts are the only agents responsible for the drift in our culture towards one of death, but they have been significant ones and had they decided such matters differently, had they acted with the judicial restraint required and traditionally recognized, the drift of the culture would at least have been slowed, if not changed.

The question becomes: Has this interaction between the culture and the law, in fact, led to a "culture of death"?

There is no doubt of the accuracy of Pope John Paul's felicitous phrase "the culture of death." In fact, it has been a "century of death," a century marked by two world wars, the first the "war to end all wars" and the second included within it the horrors of the Holocaust. One would have thought that after World War II, after all the carnage and the horror, the massive destruction of cities, the millions and millions of dead, it would have sunk into the collective consciousness of both the western and eastern worlds that a renewed respect for life was necessary. But as we all know, that has not been the history of the last half of the twentieth century. Despite the horrors of the first half, no lessons were learned, not even in the Netherlands which suf-fered so much under the Nazi's, and particularly not in the

United States, where we have so much for which to be grateful. We have seen, instead, an increasing insensitivity to life in the guise of respecting individual freedom, personal autonomy, and selfish choice.

Is the "culture of death" a valid description of the post war world? Certainly so. Why then suggest optimism? I think the reasons for some degree of optimism that we can rebuild and restore a culture of life through the law are best viewed through the prism of the recent Supreme Court decisions on assisted suicide.

Last January, the decisions in two cases issued by two different appellate courts—the Ninth Circuit in a case originating in the state of Washington and the Second Circuit in a case originating in New York—were argued before the Supreme Court. In both cases, the states had laws which prohibited doctors from providing assistance to patients who wished to commit suicide. Although both courts reached the same result by finding a constitutional right to assisted suicide (or, more precisely, by striking down laws against such assistance on constitutional grounds), they did so by different analytical means.

In the Washington state case—*Washington v. Glucksberg*—the Ninth Circuit in an en banc decision overturned on Fourteenth Amendment due process grounds the Washington state law which made it a felony to assist a suicide attempt. In doing so, it relied primarily on the right to abortion cases of *Roe v. Wade* and *Planned Parenthood v. Casey*. The Ninth Circuit said that its ruling was merely an extension of the "common thread" of the Supreme Courts' abortion decisions.

In the New York case—*Vacco v. Quill*—the Second Circuit ruled that the New York State statute against assisted suicide was unconstitutional on the grounds that it was a denial of equal protection of the laws guaranteed by the Fourteenth Amendment. The claimed equal protection denial was found because New York permitted individuals to sign waivers refusing resuscitation or to forgo artificial life supports. This was discrimination, said the Second Circuit, and thus a denial of equal protection against terminally ill people not on life support systems. In other words, the reasoning went, since persons on life support systems have a statutory right to terminate such treatment, a ban on assisted suicide discriminates against terminally ill people who are not on life support and therefore can not similarly choose a fatal withdrawal of treatment. The Second Circuit stated that "Physicians do not fulfill the role of killer by prescribing drugs to hasten death any more than they do by disconnecting life-support systems."

In two of the most important rulings in recent years, the U.S. Supreme Court, this past June, unanimously reversed both circuits' decisions and upheld the constitutionality of the laws of both New York and Washington (and implicitly the laws of most other states which have a similar reach), which forbade physician assisted suicide. Such laws violate neither the due process nor the equal protection provisions of the Constitution.

Both opinions were written by Chief Justice William Rehnquist. On behalf of the Supreme Court, the Chief Justice stated:

> There is no dispute that dying patients in Washington and New York can obtain palliative care, even when doing so would hasten their deaths. The difficulty in defining terminal illness, and the risk that a dying patients' request for assistance in ending his or her life might not be truly voluntary justifies the prohibitions on assisted suicide we uphold here.

Speaking further for the Court, Chief Justice Rehnquist rejected the notion that the constitution contains a so-called "right to die." He began his analysis "by examining our nation's history, legal traditions and practices" which led him to the conclusion that no such constitutional right exists. As regards the Washington case, he noted "our decisions lead us to conclude that the 'asserted right' to assistance in committing suicide is not a fundamental liberty interest protected by the due process clause." The consistent tradition and pattern of the states of a ban on suicide goes back deep into the common law and runs through the laws of virtually every state, said Chief Justice Rehnquist, and this consistent ban on suicide, and thus implicitly assisted suicide, expressed "the state's commitment to the protection and preservation of all human life." He went on to list the many reasons why any attempt to create an exception to this persistent protection would be unwise. He alluded to the difficulty, if not impossibility, of restricting such a right only to the terminally ill and the illogic of so restricting it. He spoke of the threat that such a right would pose to the integrity of the medical profession. He pointed out the fact that recognizing such a right would lessen the protections for the poor, the aged, those who are disabled and others who are vulnerable. And he acknowledged the need to avoid the precipitous slope that leads to euthanasia. All these reasons provided the necessary rational basis required for due process under the Fourteenth Amendment.

As regards the New York case and its equal protection argument, Chief Justice Rehnquist asserted that we must observe the distinction between removing life support systems or giving drugs with the intent to relieve pain which may have the incidental effect of shortening life, from the giving of drugs with the intent to kill. The two situations are rationally distinct.

As regards the famous mystery passage from the *Casey* decision—"at the heart of liberty is the right to define one's own concept of existence, of meaning, of the universe, and of the mystery of human life"—relied upon by Judge Reinhart in the Ninth Circuit's majority opinion in *Glucksberg*, the Chief Justice, although he did not explicitly repudiate or cast into oblivion that passage, indicated that it was inapplicable to the cases at hand because the language in *Casey* merely described "those personal activities and decisions that this court has identified as so deeply rooted in our history and traditions, or so fundamental to our concept of constitutionally ordered liberty, that they are protected by the Fourteenth Amendment." In other words, our history and tradition made it clear that suicide and assisted suicide are not part of these activities deeply rooted in our history and traditions or ones so recognized as so fundamental to our concepts of constitutionally ordered liberty.

The Court's opinion by the Chief Justice in the two cases were joined by Justices Scalia, Thomas, Kennedy and O'Connor, and there were also a number of concurring opinions.

In fact, the concurrences counted for a majority of the court. Four justices—Breyer, O'Connor, Souter, and Stevens—suggested, in various ways, that some terminally ill people in intractable pain might be able to claim at some time in the future a constitutional right to physician assistance in expediting their death. (Even the Rehnquist opinion indicates that it "does not absolutely foreclose such a claim.") In Justice O'Connor's separate concurrence,[1] she noted that although she agreed that there was "no generalized right to commit suicide" she still thought the question of whether "a mentally competent person who is experiencing great suffering" that cannot otherwise be controlled had a constitutionally based "interest in controlling his or her imminent death" was still an open one.

Without going into detail about the nuanced differences among the various concurrences, the basic point they make is a simple one—the door is still open! For anyone who wants to read a penetrating analysis of the meaning of the concurrences and the problems that they create for the future, he or she should read Professor Robert George's excellent analysis in this October's issue of the journal *First Things*. Professor George, in his usual perceptive way, also makes the point that in understanding and analyzing the Rehnquist opinion, we should be careful about being overly optimistic, since, in Professor George's phrase, "the devil, as usual, is hiding in the details" of that opinion.

In light of this analysis, what then are the reasons for optimism in terms of a change in the culture? Well, I believe there are a number of good reasons, and I will speak to them shortly. But first let me speak about the negative aspects of the decisions and the problem and challenges they present.

First, the Court made it clear that the issue is one that can be resolved by the states and this, in turn, means that we will have to continue the battle in each of the fifty state legislatures and their supreme courts, with all the uncertainty that creates. Second, a number of the justices, (I believe a majority—Stevens, Souter, Breyer, O'Connor, and Ginsburg) have left open the door for further reconsideration of this issue in the future. These justices have not decisively rejected "a right to assisted suicide in all circumstances." Although the rationale of the Court's opinion is broad enough so that the hypothetical circumstances alluded to in the concurrences are probably insufficient to bring the matter back to the Courts' attention, the possibility remains that this could occur, and one would be foolish to discount it. Third, the composition of the court is likely to change in the next few years and there is no reason to believe that the current administration is likely to appoint justices to the Supreme Court who share a philosophy of judicial restraint. Fourth, the mystery passage in the *Casey* decision asserting that "at the heart of liberty is the right to define ones own concept of existence, of meaning, of the universe, as a mystery of human life." remains alive, even if dormant. Though it appears to have been limited solely to the situation of abortion, we would be foolish to think it could not be resurrected and used in some other context. Fifth, other life related issues will be coming before the Court in the future and there is no guarantee that it will act in the same restrained fashion. The rapidly developing field of bioethics will continue to present new development which will challenge and question traditional moral principles. Such topics as supported fetal research, embryo research, prenatal screening, eugenic abortion, organ transplant, and the various concepts of "brain death" will not go away, and many will reach the courts, and this means that we cannot rest on whatever laurels we think are derived from the result in the assisted suicide cases. The bioethics field is one that is overwhelmingly secular, and it is ignorant, if not hostile, to traditional moral principles and to Judeo-Christian ethical thought. These bioethic developments, along with our society's obsession with the concept of individual autonomy, mean that there are many battles ahead to be fought with no guarantee that they will be won.

What then are the reasons for optimism regarding the opinions? First and most obvious, the result was unanimous and the correct one. Such a result sends a clear and unmistakable message. Although the majority of the members of the Court kept the door open for future challenges, the fact is that the two states' statutes involved in the cases are typical of the statutes of virtually all the states that have prohibited suicide, and thus, there is now no constitutional prohibition against them. In light of the facts of the cases and the opinion upholding the constitutionality of the statutes based on those facts, it would be very difficult for future legislators to come up with provisions that will pass constitutional muster. Although the battleground now shifts to the states, the Court's unanimous result furthermore sends a message which provides the momentum for those who support life. The reality is that assisted suicide is banned, either by state statute or judicial opinion, in most of the fifty states. Moreover, euthanasia is illegal in every state. The opinion polls also indicate that although people may initially indicate a support for assisted suicide efforts, particularly when they are packaged in the cloak of "dying with dignity" or some other euphemism, once people are forced to think about the issue seriously, that support begins to lessen. It lessens in a particularly dramatic way when people become aware of the alternatives such as better hospice care and better pain management. Even on the federal front, encouraging action has taken place. I refer to the recent passage of legislation by the Congress, legislation signed by the President into the law, prohibiting the use of federal funds for assisted suicide.

Another reason for optimism is the growing revulsion as people become more and more aware of the grim reality of abortion and assisted suicide. Look at the response of otherwise pro-abortion supporters to the partial birth abortion controversy. Many of them attempt to draw the line there. The die-hard supporters of abortion, up to and including partial birth abortions, rightfully point out, however, the illogic of such a line. They know once you acknowledge the horror of partial birth abortion, it becomes more and more difficult to defend other forms of abortion. To ban partial birth abortions does undermine the abortion rationale. The reality and the horror of current euthanasia practice in the Netherlands (despite the best efforts of the elite culture to keep that story away from the public or to discredit its truths) is also sinking into the public consciousness. One example of denial in this area can be found in Justice Souter's concurrence in the assisted suicide cases. He suggested in all seriousness that scholars seem to disagree as to what is actually going on in the Netherlands, whether, in fact, involuntary euthanasia is the order of the day. Well, anyone who has read the results of the research in this area by Professor John Keown from Cambridge University, Dr. Carlos Gomez from the University of Virginia, or Dr. Herb Hendin—all of whom who have spent time in the Netherlands doing field research and all of whom who have spent considerable time analyzing the Dutch government's own data—can have no doubt about what has happened there. It is clear that the Dutch have progressed (or, more properly, regressed) from "moving assistance in deaths, more correctly, euthanasia, from the terminally ill to the chronically ill, from those suffering physical affliction to those conflicted mentally and psychologically, and from those competent to request assistance to the incompetent, either by reason of mental inability, comatose situation, or infancy." In the same vein, the relationship between the Nazi program of involuntary euthanasia for the mentally or physically disabled and its connection with the movement today in favor of assisted suicide is now on the public agenda. In this respect, I recommend to you the books of Michael Burleigh entitled *Final Solution; Death and Deliverance: Euthanasia in Germany 1900-1945* and Henry Friedlander entitled the *Origins of Nazi Genocide: From Euthanasia to the Final Solution.*

Similarly, the assisted suicide opinions focused attention and brought into the forefront of public awareness the threat assisted suicide presents to the more vulnerable members of our society. At the bottom of the movement to legalize euthanasia is the belief that these sort of decisions should be made based on some assumption about the quality of life. Some lives have more worth than others. The efforts of significant parts of the disabled community to bring this to public attention are beginning to pay off, and more and more Americans now realize that the disabled, as well as the poor, the helpless, and the marginalized, are those who have most reason to fear the push in the direction of assisted suicide.

The recent controversy over sterilization experiments that occurred during World War II in Sweden also suggests increased and heightened public sensitivity to life concerns. There is a direct line connecting the eugenics movement, the infamous *Buck v. Bell* decision in this country ("three generations of imbeciles are enough"), the euthanasia experiments in Nazi Germany, and the movement that is going on today for the so-called "death with dignity". The a common thread is the belief that only certain members of society are fit to continue to live, and that a small elite group (mainly doctors, with the support of judges) will make these decisions and their decisions, in the final analysis, will be based on some concept, whether articulated or not, of the perceived value of the life of the individual in question.

To keep this momentum in our favor, we need to increase

our efforts to influence public opinion. We know that when the efforts are intense, there is usually a positive result. Many of you recall that both in California and Washington, states which in recent years rejected the right to assisted suicide either through initiative or referendum, the public support for some form of assisted suicide evaporated when the people were forced to grapple with the issues and confront the hard questions. (Oregon, of course, suggests a contrary experience, but even there the battle is still not over.)

The efforts of groups such as the pro-life Secretariat of the National Conference of Catholic Bishops are also important. The thoughtful work done by Richard Doerflinger, Gayle Quinn, Helen Alvare, and others are a source of inspiration for all, and their work demonstrates that successes are possible. It was through the aid and assistance of the pro-life Secretariat that we at Catholic University Law School this past spring were able to put on a very successful conference entitled *Life at Risk*. Efforts like this need to increase and multiply. We need to learn better how to communicate with our fellow citizens who have not yet made up their minds on this issue or who, if they have a predisposition, it is not a deeply embedded one. We need to present the issue in the human terms that people can readily understand. It is our narratives and stories properly presented which are the more compelling ones.

There are other important reasons to believe the momentum is on our side. We have won the intellectual battles on abortion and on assisted suicide. This is particularly so in the case in abortion. This might sound strange, since *Roe v. Wade*, as redefined in *Casey*, still stands as a constitutional principle. But no serious thinker any longer argues that what we are doing is not the killing of human beings. Moreover, the seminal thinking being done on this issue is being done by Catholic and other religious thinkers some of whom are in this room today. They really have changed the terms of the debate, and in a real sense we have won the debate. It is only slowly sinking into the culture and, of course, is barely perceptible in the media and in our elite academic institutions. But the fact remains that the arguments we have raised and the principles upon which we based these arguments are starting to prevail. As one example, I refer you to Naomi Wolf's recent book, where she makes it clear that one can not deny that aborting a baby is in fact killing it, although she goes on to say it still can be done. The awful, horrible reality of partial birth abortion has also begun to sink in. If you have any doubt that the other side is on the defensive, just look at the latest most serious argument in defense of abortion. In a recent book written by Eileen McDonagh, a political science professor at Northeastern University, it is asserted that the strongest legal case now for abortion is "self-defense". McDonagh acknowledges that the fetus is indeed a human life, but goes on to argue that just as "a woman has a right to defend herself against the rapist, she also should be able to use deadly force to expel a fetus" because if the fetus is unwanted its presence there violates her privacy. As Nat Hentoff has observed, "unlike Jonathon Swift's *Modest Proposal*, this is not a satire. It is deadly serious." Well yes, it is deadly serious, but it also demonstrates how little there is now by way of intellectual argument in defense of abortion. And what a defense it is, the mothers in society being given the right to defend themselves from all those "wanton attacking fetuses."

The intellectual victory in the field of assisted suicide is less clear, but there, too, we have reason for hope. Even the liberal intellectual community is divided on the issue, and it appears, based on the experiences in California and Washington, that when people are forced to confront the reality of what is going on, they change their views from a superficial acceptance of the idea of assisted suicide because of the need for "death with dignity" to a heightened perception of the dangers, risks and threats posed by it.

In addition, we have the intellectual foundation or framework in which the important questions in the future can best be addressed. It is our tradition of natural law, and our belief in the objectivity and universality of moral norms, which provides the necessary grounding for recognizing the inherent dignity and worth of every individual and which offers the best framework of the construction of a just society and political order. The luminous and profound writings of Pope John Paul II have done much to enrich our intellectual tradition. As Father Richard Neuhaus has observed in the October 1997 issue of *First Things*, the Pope's strong affirmation of truth and objectivity and of a morality discovered through a vibrant natural law, his passionate attacks and opposition to the culture of death, his determination to encourage people of good will to work together in an effective ecumenical fashion, and his friendly but constructively critical conversation with capitalism, all enrich the tradition that we represent. Father Neuhaus went on to state:

> But one can make the case that, as a world force, Christianity offers the only coherent, comprehensive, and compelling vision of the human project.

Moreover, one of the dominant trends of the next century, the twenty-first century, is going to be religion, and that is another reason for optimism. Marxism is clearly discredited and all but dead. The Enlightenment—referred to by Peter Gay in his seminal work as the "Rise of Modern Paganism"—is uttering its last, dying gasps, having demonstrated beyond all reasonable doubt that it is bereft of a firm moral foundation. The hollowness and emptiness of materialism and secularism is apparent to all. And the destructive effects of a complete, unfettered, and unchecked individual autonomy is also obvious to all. It is religion—particularly Roman Catholicism, Evangelical Christianity, and a resurgent Orthodox Judaism in this country, and Catholicism and Islam in the international sphere—that will be the dominant force in the next century.

Although this appears a reason to celebrate, we must remind

ourselves that it does not mean that only good things can happen. Again, Father Neuhaus wisely reminds us that the fact that the next century may "be religious is not necessarily good news. Religion is as riddled with the possibilities of mischief as any other dimension of the human condition." We are well advised to keep Father Neuhaus' words in mind before we get too optimistic about success or triumph. It is a never ending, always shifting battle, and if recent history teaches us anything, it is not to be overconfident about the possibility of success. On the other hand, we do have—and I don't mean to be flip about this—God on our side. We are doing God's work, imperfectly sometimes, ineffectively other times, but confidently all times. As Pope John Paul II has urged "Be not afraid!"—words to inspire and give confidence to us all.

Finally we need to remind ourselves that the culture is not static or unchanging and neither is law. Each is dynamic and each can be shaped and influenced and informed in many different ways. Each is contingent on the other. Our opponents control the basic institutions that most influence the culture— the media, the universities, the technology, and the law—but we have them on the run—well, perhaps not the run, but at least they are starting to walk away, slowly. We are constantly reminded these days that we are a multicultural society and that we must be sensitive to all diverse cultures. Well, we are part of the culture too, and we need to remind the rest of the culture that we have a place at the table and we will not be elbowed aside. It is time for us to make "our necessities felt" in the culture and in the law. When we do that, then we can speak in a more meaningful fashion of building of culture of life through the law.

Please note: because this was a speech, footnotes were not included

Note

1. This all gets very technical and convoluted—Justice
    O'Connor joined the Rehnquist opinion which was
    also joined by Scalia, Thomas and Kennedy, but she
    additionally filed a separate concurring opinion,
    which was joined by Justice Ginsburg and also by
    Justice Breyer in part; Justice Breyer, in turn, filed his
    own separate concurring opinion as did Justices
    Souter and Stevens.

Building the Culture of Life Through Law: A Response

Helen Alvare
National Conference of Catholic Bishops
Washington, D.C.

The larger percentage of audiences I address are pro-life. Considering that a lot of dissidents come to my talks (I invite them in) or that I am speaking in a debate situation, the percentage of pro-lifers is probably 60 percent. Regarding debates, I encourage a diversity of views at abortion debates in any university setting, including Catholic universities. The reason is that I want to encourage the dissenters to come to the talk. So, my observations come from both of these crowds.

One of the first observations I have regarding the law's influence among the people I meet is their incredible cynicism about the law, and for that matter, about legislation and politics as well. This attitude flows, I would say, primarily from the *Roe v. Wade* decision and the use of the language and reasoning of *Roe* in the "death and dying" cases. One example of this is that in 1973 the Supreme Court was referring to what was growing in a woman's *womb* as "potential life." What a joke! *Everybody* knew at the time before, during, and after the proceedings that there was a consensus within the scientific community that life began at conception and is continuous until death. For the justices to say that they could not identify what was growing in the mother's womb and to describe it as "potential life"–words which everyone knew were made-up—is what John Paul II refers to as "failing to call things by their proper name." This was done in the name of reaching a particular result. The Court clearly understood that it was making up what it needed to in order to attain its end, in the same way that the language of "pre-embryo" has come into vogue recently in order to reach a certain end, and in the same way that Planned Parenthood is changing the language of what pregnancy is when they describe the morning after pill as contraception, and not abortion. Everyone understands that our Supreme Court refused to acknowledge what everyone knew, namely that the thing is question was human life and that human life has begun when abortions are committed.

Another example: people are coming to understand that both the courts' and legislators' insistence that we need a health exception for abortion is also a medical falsehood; that there is not a situation in which you have to kill an unborn child to remove him or her from the mother. Today, "health of the mother" abortions usually mean the children are disabled. But abortion does not make the mother healthier and we know it does not make the child healthier. That has come out most recently in the partial-birth abortion debate in which a group of 600 doctors, the Physicians Ad Hoc Coalition for Truth, has said it again and again and again, on Capitol Hill, around the country and in advertisements, that it is not necessary to kill to deliver, let alone, by a method so brutal as partial birth abortion.

More falsehood is found in the euthanasia decisions, the most recent ones being *Vacco v. Quill* and *Washington v. Glucksburg*. There the Court casually dismissed the *Casey* definition of a constitutional liberty interest, by saying, "Oh well, we never meant for that to be a definition." This is ridiculous! (The Dean nicely referred to this passage from *Casey* as the "mystery passage." I am not so nice. When I speak about it I refer to it as the "wacko passage"). In order to point out the absurdity of the passage, I often take high school and college students through the exercise of trying to imagine what it would be like if each one of them could live together for a single day according to their "view of the universe." That is, how would they all behave if they lived merely according to the *idea* of the real world that was in their head, according to what their *personal* truth was, according to what the universe looked like in their own head. Truly, it is the most ridiculous passage. And the way the Supreme Court dismissed it in their euthanasia cases was really the Supreme Court saying that they went out of bounds and that they just have to draw some lines now. They said at the conclusion—after supposedly distinguishing that description from what they meant as a "liberty interest"—that many of the rights and liberties protected by the due process clause, such as personal autonomy, do not warrant the sweeping conclusion that any and all important, intimate and personal decisions are so protected. Why not? They really never made that clear. The magazine *Policy Review* wrote that what the court stated was, if effect, "Well you know, you just gotta put a limit to freedom somewhere." If everyone would have understood the court in that way, then everyone would have understood that the court had made a mistake, and the court was not willing to acknowledge that.

I find the audiences I encounter also very cynical about politics. And I believe that there is no coincidence that abortion is the issue that gave rise to that famous and ridiculous phrase, "personally opposed, but…" Everyone knows what is being said by that phrase—which is, "Either I do or I do not have personal misgivings about abortion, but it is not politically wise at this time for me to vote against it. Rather, I will say that I am morally opposed to it, but will not only vote to keep it legal for nine months for any reason, but I would also like you to pay for it." This is, as you know, at the very heart of hypocrisy in politics. And I do not believe that it is a coincidence that the abortion issue, which started in a lie and continues through lies, is the political issue that gave rise to that ridiculous political phrase.

I find people actually have, in many ways, less respect for law than I believe is healthy for them. But, it is also unhealthy when the law as an institution loses that much of its moral force, thus losing so much of its potential for doing good. People tend to believe that the Supreme Court is out of touch. "Out of touch" is a nice way of putting it; they believe that the Supreme Court is so elite and far removed from them and acting on its own interest, that it has nothing much to say to the people I am referring to, and much to say that would simply offend them or make them laugh.

You will also find in the culture, as a result of the infamous life and death cases, and most profoundly because of *Roe*, an inculturation of the words "choice" and "freedom." Words that turn us away from the idea that it is important for us to investigate the content of our actions, or the content of the offered choices. Having lots of choices is portrayed as a *per se*, good, maybe even a moral good. Whether it is AT&T's "the right choice," "Personal Choice Banking," or "Healthy Choice dinners," it is evident that in using the word "choice" none of the above references focus us on such things as whether any of the food is good, or whether any of the calling options are right, but solely on the fact that they can fit your lifestyle. It is not too much to say that it affirms the idea that truth is of no matter; that whether anything is particularly good or not, is not of any particular concern, just whether it fits one's lifestyle. That is deemed as good in itself.

Another observation that I find inculturated particularly by *Roe*, and in particular by the Ninth Circuit euthanasia decision which claims to rely on *Roe*, is the idea that, in considering who is and who is not valuable, people who are more dependant are nothing but a burden to us and hold no possibility for being gifts to us. Children are primarily included in this idea. One line in particular from *Roe* exemplifies this. The first time I read it I thought it was awful. Reading it after I had children made me laugh myself silly. *Roe's* description of motherhood is as follows: "The detriment the state would impose upon the pregnant women by denying this choice (abortion) is altogether apparent. Specific and direct harm, medically diagnosable in early pregnancy may be involved, maternity or additional off-spring may force upon the woman a distressful life and future, psychological harm may be imminent, mental and physical health may be taxed by childcare. There is also the distress for all concerned with the unwanted child and the problem of bringing the child into a family unable, psychologically and otherwise, to care for it..." And the passage goes on and on and on.

After I spent my first year with a daughter we casually referred to as "Momar", short for Momar Kadafi, because she held us hostage with her crying, I went back and read the above passage from *Roe* and thought, "Oh no! Psychological harm could come from child bearing." And I realized that what *Roe* described is on a continuum with every family. Everyone is going to lose sleep, everyone is going to worry about the finances, everyone is going to be psychologically taxed. Note, however, that when they described child rearing this is all they had to say. It was not just what they said that struck me, but that this was *all* they had to say about children. And you can see the inculturating power of *Roe's* language. Children are portrayed only as a burden. I say this even though there is a resurgence of what I would call a militant championing of motherhood, done so because mothers feel they have to in the midst of this sort of culture.

I recently read two things which really struck me relating to the state of our popular culture in the wake of *Roe*. The kind of things that our 17 year old daughters are likely swallowing at a high pace. The first was a copy of *Glamour Magazine* . (Do not ever read *Glamour Magazine* except if you are doing research. It is very depressing and, really, I urge you to keep it out of your house.) I happened to read it last month when I was in the Bismarck airport for a 24-hour stretch and I picked it up because it was all there was. I had just finished *Story of a Soul* by Therése of Lisieux, and I was out of reading material. The magazine was composed of 21 separate little stories that were composed of tiny paragraphs and some lengthier ones, all written and geared to their ideal audience of 17 year old girls. The content of the articles included such things as how to have sex, how to have an orgasm, how to have sex so long that you break your bed, what kind of underwear to wear, what the new contraception out there is, and what are the horrible things that pro-lifers are doing at abortion clinics. And that was just a sampling from the 21 small articles. What was their feature article? An article by a woman in which she sought to explain so as to render inculpable the last wave of young women to kill their newborns. And what was her reason? She wrote that pregnancy and child bearing were for these young women such a mental disaster, such a physical disaster, such an awful thing, that these girls were rendered temporarily insane when they found out they were pregnant or saw the baby. Sex is a toy, children are monsters who can drive you temporarily insane, pregnancy is alien to our bodies and to women...if you really look hard at the magazine, this is what it is saying. And I have seen this before. I pick one of these magazines about once a year to make sure that nothing has changed.

A Planned Parenthood director wrote a letter to the *Wall Street Journal* that some of you may have seen recently. It was on the occasion of one of the neonaticides in New Jersey. The letter basically contained a similar message: the young girl confronted with pregnancy and the birth of her child, "the Prom mom," was just not prepared to face this, it overwhelmed her. And so, she is not to blame for the killing, but rather, and I quote, "...those people who give abortion a bad name," in effect, pro-lifers are to blame for this killing!

One final and related trend that I find in my mind is the idea, (and this is closely related to the prior one) that women are really weak victims. Abortion law has given rise to the idea that we are weak, particularly when faced with our natural fertility, child bearing, and motherhood, and that we can do nothing else but kill them. The idea is that when it comes to abortion, it is out of our hands; we are powerless, and our fertility is a terrible curse. Only abortion can free us. The article by the Planned Parenthood director in the *Wall Street Journal* is a perfect example of this trend. It is ironic that this idea is occurring at the same time when women are in the throes of a struggle to assert how powerful we are, that we are as well educated, and we are equal. I frankly think the notion that women are weak victims when it comes to pregnancy undermines this struggle. If you are so weak that you cannot face your own body and your own offspring then how strong can we be as women? It always raises that question.

In conclusion, I would say that I have been very disturbed by the influence of abortion jurisprudence on the law, especially on college campuses. Very much so. And also they are present among what I would call the more elite segments of Catholics. However, in the end, I see tremendous reason for hope in one thing: basic evangelization. The great thing about evangelization is that you do not have to spend your time with people refuting each of the above arguments. Once they are truly evangelized to the God of Life, to the Creator, to the Gospel of Life, once they are evangelized in that regard and have a personal relationship with God so that they understand who human beings are supposed to be, then all this other stuff is swept away and they understand pro-life arguments easily!

Index

A Short History of the Fellowship of Catholic Scholars

The Fellowship of Catholic Scholars came into existence in 1977 "in order to serve Jesus Christ better by helping one another in our work and by putting our abilities more fully at the service of the Catholic faith."

The Fellowship was not an accidental creation. It came into being as a result of a question put to several of its founders by Gabriel Cardinal Garrone, then Prefect of the Congregation of Catholic Education: Is there no other voice for Cathlolic higher education in the United States other than the officers of the National Catholic Education Association? At the time the Holy See was having difficulty getting NCEA's university department (presently the *Association of Catholic Colleges and Universities*) to adopt norms by which their Catholicity might be nudged by Church authority. Although Notre Dame's Fr. Theodore Hesburgh was often a prominent spokesman for their independence, the chief antagonists of the Holy See on this issue were Jesuits. After a study was made of selected University personnel in the United States the Fellowship came into being in the Spring of 1977, committed to "the defined teachings of the Catholic Church and those teachings proclaimed by the Church's ordinary and universal magisterium."

The first President was Fr. Ronald Lawler, OFM Cap, assisted by Vice-Presidents Joseph Fessio, SJ, Dr. James Hitchcock, and Fr. Earl Weis, SJ. Msgr. George A. Kelly became executive secretary. The Fellowship was sponsored by John Cardinal Carberry, Archbishop of St. Louis. The first convention was held in Kansas City, Missouri from April 28-30, 1978, and Cardinal William Baum provided the keynote address on "The Teaching Office of Bishops." The Fellowship's Statement of Purpose was drafted by Germain Grisez and Fr. Lawler, and the By-laws by Fr. Henry V. Sattler, CSSR.

In subsequent years the Fellowship has given public support to papal documents from *Humanae Vitae* to *Ex Corde Ecclesiae*, and has censured errant theologians such as Hans Küng and Charles Curran. However, the Fellowship has focused mainly on encouraging the active participation in research and writing helpful to the Church's work of evangelization. Publications by Fellowship members include *The Ethical Dimension of Political Life* by Francis Canavan, SJ, *The Social Teaching of Vatican II*, by Rodger Charles, SJ, *Mrs. Seton*, by Joseph I. Dirvin, CM, *The Way of the Lord Jesus* by Germain Grisez, *The Treasury of Catholic Wisdom* by John Hardon, SJ, *Catholicism and Modernity* by James Hitchcock, *Covenantal Theology* by Donald Keefe, SJ, *The Battle for the American Church* by George A. Kelly, *The Teaching of Christ* by Ronald Lawler et al., *The Nature and Meaning of Chastity* by William May, *The Gift of Infallibility* by James O'Connor, *The Christian Meaning of Human Sexuality* by Paul Quay, SJ, *Catechesis and Controversies* by Michael Wrenn, and many, many others.

The Fellowship has also provided scholarly assistance to individual bishops, and has encouraged and developed interrelationships among various Catholic insitutions of higher education, religious associations, media enterprises, and other Catholic apostolates and activist organizations.

Each year the Fellowship awards the Cardinal Wright Award in recognition of an individual who has provided outstanding scholarship to the Church. The Fellowship has also awarded the Cardinal O'Boyle Award for unusual service to the universal Church, and the Founders Award recognizes outstanding work on behalf of the Church in the intellectual apostolate.

In 1992 the Fellowship entered a new phase of development with the election of Professors Ralph McInerny and Gerard Bradley, both of the University of Notre Dame, as president and vice-president respectively. In 1994 Dean Jude Dougherty of Catholic University of America succeeded to the office of executive secretary and treasurer, replacing Joseph Scottino, former President of Gannon University, who was a founding member and treasurer since 1977.

Msgr. George A. Kelly

Fellowship of Catholic Scholars

STATEMENT OF PURPOSE

Applicants for membership should first study the
purposes of the Fellowship.

These purposes may be stated as follows:

1.   We Catholic scholars in various disciplines join in fellowship in order to serve Jesus Christ better by helping one another in our work and by putting our abilities more fully at the service of the Catholic faith.

2.   We wish to form a fellowship of scholars who see their intellectual work as an expression of the service that they owe to God. To Him we give thanks for our Catholic faith and for every opportunity He gives us to serve that faith.

3.   We wish to form a fellowship of Catholic scholars open to the work of the Holy Spirit within the Church. Thus we wholeheartedly accept and support the renewal of the Church of Christ undertaken by Pope John XXIII shaped by Vatican II and carried on by succeeding pontiffs.

4.   We accept as the rule of our life and thought the entire faith of the Catholic Church. This we see not merely in solemn definitions but in the ordinary teaching of the Pope and those bishops in union with him, and also embodied in those modes of worship and ways of Christian life and practice, of the present as of the past, which have been in harmony with the teaching of St. Peter's successors in the See of Rome.

5.   The questions raised by contemporary thought must be considered with courage and dealt with in honesty. We will seek to do this, faithful to the truth always guarded in the Church by the Holy Spirit and sensitive to the needs of the family of faith. We wish to accept a responsibility which a Catholic scholar may not evade: to assist everyone, so far as we are able, to personal assent to the mystery of Christ as made manifest through the lived faith of the Church, His Body, and through the active charity without which faith is dead.

6.   To contribute to this sacred work, our fellowship will strive to:
    · come to know and welcome all who share our purpose;

    · make known to one another our various competencies and interests;

    · share our abilities with one another unstintingly in our efforts directed to our common purpose;

    · cooperate in clarifying the challenges which must be met;

· help one another to evaluate critically the variety of responses which are proposed to these challenges;

· communicate our suggestions and evaluation to members of the Church who might find them helpful;

· respond to requests to help the Church in its task of guarding the faith as inviolable and defending it with fidelity;

· help one another to work through, in scholarly and prayerful fashion and without public dissent, any problem which may arrise from magisterial teaching.

7.   With the grace of God for which we pray, we hope to assist the whole Church to understand its own identity more clearly, to proclaim the joyous Gospel of Jesus more confidently, and to carry out its redemptive mission of all humankind more effectively.

CLASSES OF AFFILIATION

According to the **By-Laws**, the Fellowship has the following classes of affiliation:

1.   **All those affiliated** in any way with the Fellowship, who wish to give the Fellowship spiritual, moral, and financial support, and who have been duly elected to their class of affiliation.

2.   **Regular members** are those who, in addition to the qualifications mentioned in 1., are persons (a) with an earned doctorate, or the equivalent thereof; (b) regularly engage in scholarly work, as evidenced by scholarly-publications or in some other suitable manner; (c) intend active involvement in the organization, administration, or operation of the Fellowship, and in the pursuit of its goals and purposes.

3.   **Associates** of the Fellowship of Catholic Scholars are those who have qualifications mentioned in 1. but do not have all those called for in 2.

APPLICATION FOR MEMBERSHIP

If you have read and agree with the principles and purposes of the Fellowship of Catholic Scholars and would like to be considered for membership, please send your name, title, organization, address, and phone number to:

Dr. Jude P. Dougherty
Department of Philosophy
Catholic University of America
Washington, D.C. 20064